# Making Marvelous Music Boxes

by Sharon Ganske

Sterling Publishing Co., Inc.  New York
A Sterling/Chapelle Book

CHAPELLE:

Jo Packham, Owner

Cathy Sexton, Editor

Staff:   Malissa Boatwright, Sara Casperson, Rebecca Christensen, Amber Hansen, Holly Hollingsworth, Susan Jorgensen, Susan Laws, Amanda McPeck, Barbara Milburn, Pat Pearson, Leslie Ridenour, Cindy Rooks, Cindy Stoeckl, Ryanne Webster, and Nancy Whitley

HAZEN PHOTOGRAPHY:   Kevin Dilley, Photographer

If you have any questions or comments or would like information on specialty products featured in this book, please contact: Chapelle, Ltd., Inc., P.O. Box 9252, Ogden, UT  84409 • (801) 621-2777 • (801) 621-2788 Fax

Library of Congress Cataloging-in-Publication Data
Ganske, Sharon.
    Making marvelous music boxes  /  by Sharon Ganske.
        p.    cm.
    "A Sterling / Chapelle book."
    Includes index.
    ISBN 0-8069-4281-9
    1.  Music box — Construction.   I.  Title.
    ML1066.G36  1996
    786.6'51923--dc20                                        95-49846
                                                             CIP
                                                             MN


10  9  8  7  6  5  4  3  2  1

Published by Sterling Publishing Company, Inc.
387 Park Avenue South, New York, NY  10016
© 1996 by Chapelle Ltd.
Distributed in Canada by Sterling Publishing
c/o Canadian Manda Group, One Atlantic Avenue, Suite 105
Toronto, Ontario, Canada  M6K 3E7
Distributed in Great Britain and Europe by Cassell PLC
Wellington House, 125 Strand, London WC2R 0BB, England
Distributed in Australia by Capricorn Link (Australia) Pty Ltd.
P.O. Box 6651, Baulkham Hills, Business Centre, NSW 2153, Australia
Printed in China
All Rights Reserved

Sterling ISBN 0-8069-4281-9

## To Jared & Jessica ... The music in my life...

### Thank you to:

My husband, Tracy, for all the help in creating this book: the dinners you cooked, the dishes you washed, the floors you vacuumed, the ways you entertained the kids, the honest opinions, the good ideas, the help cutting out and preparing the wood and, especially, for the 107 holes you drilled! Remember, I love you the mostest!

My mom, Sonia Burgett, for base painting and dry brushing some of the projects and, especially, for helping with Jared and Jessi!

My sister, Cathy Burket, for running all over town with endless shopping lists and, especially, for always coming back!

Areta Bingham, for painting the clown's face for the "Be a Clown" music box.

Jo Packham, for this opportunity!

And, a special remembrance to the late Michael Richeson for making the porcelain doll used with the "Thank Heaven" music box.

### About the author:

Sharon resides with her husband and two children in Riverdale, Utah. She has always enjoyed any craft, and also enjoys being a "stay-at-home" mom. Sharon is a part-time designer for a design company in Ogden, Utah, and her designs and creations have appeared in several publications. This book features her designs exclusively, and is the first book of its kind for this artist.

# Table of Contents

# Before Beginning

## Music Box Titles

The titles for the music boxes in this book are named with the titles of the songs that were used as the musical movements. The song titles seem to help create the themes for the music boxes. Feel free to replace any of the melodies with other favorites.

## Levels of Ability

The music boxes in this book were created with all crafters in mind. None of them are prohibitive because of skill level — a little practice using the techniques outlined in the General Instructions will assure confidence in attempting any of these music boxes. In the Table of Contents, the music boxes have been categorized from simplest ♪, to moderate ♪, to most difficult ♪.

## Decorative Accessories

Looking for the various decorative accessories to use with a music box can be as much fun as actually creating the music box. The "perfect" trinket is often-times a challenge to find, however, if a particular decorative accessory used in these music boxes cannot be found, simply find a replacement to go along with the theme of the music box.

Many of the decorative accessories used with these music boxes were miniatures that are available in most crafts stores. Key chains are a great source for finding some of the miniatures used, for example, the saddle in "Country Roads" on page 67.

Many times it is easier to find figurines that are prepainted. If the figurines are not painted with desired colors, they can simply be re-painted. The only time this will not work is when they have a glazed finish.

Decorative accessories can also be viewed as individual works of art. If a particular accessory cannot be found, create one. For example, the stack toy and the gumball machine that were used in "My Favorite Things" on page 117. The stack toy was created with wooden buttons and a wooden bead — brightly painted and glued together. The gumball machine was created with a wooden candle cup and a wooden knob — painted solid first and then the details added.

## Musical Movements

Musical movements can be found at most crafts stores, but the accessories are oftentimes difficult to find. Most ceramic shops can order the accessories. If questions about specialty products featured in this book arise, please contact Chapelle, Ltd., Inc., P.O. Box 9252, Ogden, UT 84409.

It is important to know that different manufacturers of musical movements and musical movement accessories make their own molds for producing these parts. Therefore, it is crucial to check all parts before beginning to make any of these music boxes. For example, all winding keys, key extenders, and threaded-shafts should be checked to make sure they fit together properly, as well as to make sure the recommended drill hole size will work with the accessories. Keep in mind that left-hand threaded parts only fit onto other left-hand threaded parts. Generally, all musical movement accessories are left-hand threaded.

Read the sections on Musical Movements, Movement Accessories, and General Instructions before beginning. This will help describe and explain specific musical movement parts, as well as give an overview of the basic techniques used in making these music boxes.

# ♪ Musical Movements

### 18-Note Key-Wind

These are the most commonly used musical movements when making music boxes. They are available in a number of different song titles.

To add many kinds of motion, 18-note key-wind musical movements can be used with animation accessories by inserting a left-hand threaded-shaft into the special accessory hole on the side of the musical movement.

Overall dimensions of the musical movements measure $2^1/_8$" x $1^7/_8$" x $1^1/_{16}$", and they wind from the bottom.

These musical movements are also available in "clear tone" — the housing over the top of the musical movement is clear so the musical mechanism can be observed while it is playing. Refer to "Clear Tone" musical movements.

### Double-Action

These musical movements always have a turntable attached. The turntable rotates in one direction, while three small disks on top of the turntable independently spin figurines back and forth.

Most often, double-action musical movements come complete with all necessary parts, plus a standard 18-note key-wind musical movement.

The width of the turntable on the musical movements is $3^1/_4$" at its widest point, and they wind from the bottom.

These musical movements were used in two music boxes in this book: "Raindrops Keep Falling" on page 38 in which the "bugs" spin and "Funeral March of the Marionettes" on page 79 in which the "bats" spin while the turntables rotate.

### Magnetic Swing Arm

These musical movements rotate in a circle underneath the music box lid. By gluing a figurine to the top of a magnet and placing the magnet on the music box lid, the figurine will dance and spin in a circular-motion because of the magnetic swing arm musical movement under the top of the lid.

Most often, magnetic swing arm musical movements come complete with all necessary parts, plus a standard 18-note key-wind musical movement.

Overall dimensions of these musical movements measure 2" x $1^3/_4$" x $1^3/_4$", and they wind from the bottom. They are available in a limited number of different song titles.

The magnetic swing arm musical movement was used in "Peter Cottontail" on page 36.

# Miniature

These miniature musical movements are 18-note key-wind musical movements, but they do not have a special accessory hole. Therefore, no animation accessories can be used. However, miniature turntables are available to fit the winding-key shaft on miniature musical movements. They come in a number of different song titles, but not as many are available as in the standard 18-note key-wind musical movements.

Overall dimensions of miniature musical movements measure $1^{11}/_{16}$" x $1^3/_8$" x $^9/_{16}$", and they wind from the bottom.

These musical movements were used in four music boxes in this book: "Love Story" on page 26, "Thank Heaven" on page 41, "Teddy Bears Picnic" on page 52, and "Silent Night" on page 96. Because of the space limitations in these music boxes, the miniature musical movements fit snugly into position. When using these musical movements, a miniature winding key must be used.

# Electronic Miniature

These electronic musical movements play by the simple touch of a finger. Their batteries generally last up to 10,000 plays and replacement batteries are available. They come in a number of different song titles.

Overall dimensions of electronic miniature musical movements measure $1^3/_8$" diameter x $^1/_4$" high. No winding key is required.

These musical movements were used in two music boxes in this book: "Brahms Lullaby" on page 42 and "Hawaiian Wedding Song" on page 57.

Using the assembly instructions for making a pouch on page 58, sew one into just about anything. Place an electronic miniature musical movement into the pouch and enjoy the melody at the touch of a finger. The musical movement should be placed inside the pouch so that it can be removed before laundering. Of course, using industrial-strength glue, an electronic miniature musical movement can be glued to just about anything as well.

# Clear Tone

Clear tone musical movements are 18-note key-wind musical movements, but the housing over the top of the musical movement is clear so the musical mechanism inside can be observed while the music is playing. They are available in a number of different song titles.

Unlike standard 18-note key-wind musical movements, clear tone musical movements cannot be used with animation accessories because there is no special accessory hole on the side.

Overall dimensions of these musical movements measure $2^3/_8$" x 2" x $1^3/_{16}$", which makes them slightly larger than standard 18-note key-wind musical movements. They wind from the bottom.

The 18-note key-wind clear tone musical movement was used in "Wind Beneath My Wings" on page 44. If a clear tone musical movement had not been used, covering the musical movement inside the box would give a more finished look. Refer to "When You Wish Upon A Star" on page 104.

# Movement Accessories

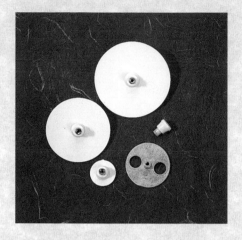

## Shafts & Extenders

Left-hand threaded-shafts are inserted into the special accessory hole on the side of the 18-note key-wind musical movement. Once a left-hand threaded-shaft is inserted, it becomes permanent and cannot be removed.

Left-hand threaded turntables and animation accessories can be attached to a left-hand threaded-shaft or shaft extender. In this case, the turntable can never be used as the winding key.

Key extenders are used to extend the length of the winding key. Left-hand threaded-shaft extenders are used to extend the height of the left-hand threaded-shaft and the height of the top-mount rotation assembly. Both extenders are available in several different lengths and can be combined to get any length necessary.

## Animation

There are several animation accessories available to fit the 18-note key-wind musical movements. A left-hand threaded-shaft is required when using these animation accessories, except when using a top-mount rotation assembly, as it is already attached.

The waggie shaft is covered with an accordion sleeve, which allows the waggie shaft to rotate inside the sleeve instead of inside the figure. The motion is circular, but the shaft also tilts backward and forward as it revolves.

The circular-motion rod is easily bent to create an orbital flying motion. A flat pad at the rod tip provides a surface to glue figurines to.

The top-mount rotation assembly allows animation at the top, while also allowing a winding key at the bottom.

## Turntables

Turntables come in several different sizes, including miniature. They come in clear plastic, opaque plastic, and metal.

Left-hand threaded turntables are available to fit a left-hand threaded-shaft or shaft extender. Left-hand threaded turntables also fit on top of the top-mount rotation assembly. Turntables can be used as winding keys when figurines are glued to them, unless a left-hand threaded turntable is being used.

When a turntable is attached to the winding-key shaft, it must become the winding key.

If using a plastic turntable, and the turntable is larger than the base of the figurine being glued to it, it can be cut down and sanded so it does not extend from underneath the figurine.

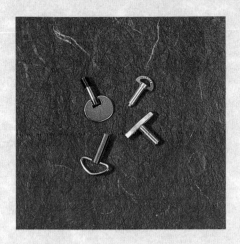

## Winding Keys

Winding keys must be used with all musical movements, unless a turntable is used in its place.

Winding keys are available in either brass- or nickel-plated finishes and come in several different sizes.

The T-bar winding key is the most commonly used and is the easiest winding key to grip while winding. It is recognizable by its shape.

The triangle ring winding key allows the ring to fold down against the shaft, but is not quite as easy to wind.

The miniature winding key is used for miniature musical movements and is very difficult to wind because of its size.

There is also a child-proof safety winding key. Once this winding key is installed in the musical movement, it becomes permanent and cannot be removed. It is recommended that these winding keys always be used when a child will have access to the music box.

## Accessory Shaft Washers

Accessory shaft washers are used on the outside of the musical movement housing by simply being slipped over the special accessory shaft before the accessory is installed. It is recommended using the washers when plush toys or dolls are used. The accessory shaft washer helps prevent the fibers from getting caught in the special accessory hole and getting wrapped around the special accessory shaft.

This accessory was not featured in this book.

## Cranks

Cranks are used to produce a variety of motions, including swinging, pumping, sawing, rocking, and up and down motion.

Crank handles must be used with an accessory shaft, however, some styles have the accessory shafts attached.

This accessory was not featured in this book.

## Rocking Action

The rocking action assembly fits into the special accessory hole on the 18-note key-wind musical movement. This assembly comes with the left-hand threaded-shaft already attached. The rocker arm comes attached to the crank handle and special animation shaft. The rocking motion is perfect for chairs and horses.

This accessory was not featured in this book.

## Revolving Displays

The revolving display fits all 18-note key-wind musical movements. It fits into the winding-key shaft on the musical movement.

The revolving display usually has a bright brass-plated finish and measures $7^5/8$" high. It holds objects up to $4^1/4$" long.

The revolving display serves as the winding unit and screws onto the musical movement.

Because no left-hand threaded-shaft is necessary, the revolving display can be attached to an 18-note key-wind clear tone musical movement.

This accessory was not featured in this book.

## Musical Mobile Holder Cases

Try making a musical mobile for a baby's crib using any 18-note key-wind musical movement enclosed in a musical mobile holder case. Musical movements and holder cases are sold separately. However, there are some available as one unit.

This musical movement is available with the winding key built-in. When wound, the "hook" revolves while the music plays.

It comes in white plastic. The case is easy to assemble and comes with the mounting hardware. Overall dimensions of the case measure $2^3/4$" diameter x $4^1/2$" long.

This accessory was not featured in this book.

# General Instructions

## Antiquing

When antiquing a flat surface, use an old paintbrush or, if preferred, an old clean rag. Apply a small amount of antiquing gel to flat surface (or rag). Brushing in the same direction, brush onto surface, covering completely and removing as much as desired. Do not go back over areas once they have begun to dry or a "smudge" look will appear. Using an old clean rag, wipe off as much as desired. Allow to dry thoroughly.

When antiquing a textured surface, use an old paintbrush. Apply a moderate amount of antiquing gel to a small section of textured surface, making sure the antiquing gel is in all cracks and crevices. Using an old clean rag, wipe off as much as desired, leaving more antiquing gel in cracks and crevices.

Continue antiquing small sections at a time. Do not go back over areas once they have begun to dry. Allow to dry thoroughly.

If antiquing is too dark, use a cleaning solvent on a clean, soft rag to carefully wipe it off. Remove as much as desired.

## Découpaging

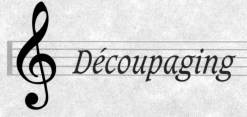

When découpaging, make sure surfaces are smooth and clean. Apply a thin, even layer of découpage to a small section of surface, using an old paintbrush or, if preferred, a sponge brush. Press paper or fabric firmly onto découpage and rub gently, but firmly, to remove air bubbles and wrinkles. Continue découpaging until entire surface is covered. Allow to dry overnight.

Apply a second coat of découpage over entire surface. Allow to dry until surface is clear. Apply as many layers as necessary to achieve desired look.

For a textured finish, apply a thick coat of découpage similar to an artist's brush strokes. For a build-up finish, apply at least five coats of découpage, allowing to dry thoroughly between coats. Wet-sand using #400 sandpaper until smooth. Wipe with a clean, damp cloth. If desired, apply more coats and wet-sand again.

## Dry Brushing

Dry brushing is a very simple technique to add depth. When dry brushing, use a stiff round paintbrush, stiff flat paintbrush, or, if preferred, a stenciling brush. Dip the brush in acrylic paint. Wipe the brush on a paper towel until there is only a very small amount of paint left on the brush.

Lightly brush over area, always brushing in the same direction so paint adheres to raised surfaces. If paint appears too light, simply add another coat.

The trick to dry brushing is making sure there is absolutely no water in the brush. If dry brushing with more than one color is necessary, wipe brush on a paper towel — do not wash it. Once first paint color seems to be adequately removed, dip brush in the second color of acrylic paint and repeat process.

When dry brushing on ceramics appears too dark, allow acrylic paint to dry thoroughly. Paint the surface with another coat of base color, allow to dry thoroughly, and try dry brushing again.

When dry brushing on fabrics, such as velvet, dry-brush small areas at a time and apply it very lightly. Once the paint dries it cannot be removed.

## Laminating

Laminating should be done over waxed paper and a clean, wet washcloth should be readily available to wash hands. Laminating is similar to wallpapering. Thin-bodied Tacky glue is used and is applied with an old paintbrush or, if preferred, a sponge brush or mini trim roller. When laminating ribbon, apply ribbon to side of box, aligning it with bottom edge. When laminating fabric, apply fabric to side of box, overlapping 1/4", unless otherwise indicated.

Apply a moderate, even layer of glue to surface. Beginning at the back center of box — marked with a seam — wrap ribbon or fabric around the box, making sure to remove air bubbles and wrinkles. For fabric, fold and glue under 1/3" at center back and glue finished edges down. Apply glue to 1/2" outer edge on bottom of box. Wrap excess fabric around and press to bottom of box, smoothing out as many wrinkles as possible. Glue and wrap excess fabric at top of box to the inside top edge of box. Allow to dry thoroughly.

To laminate circles, lay fabric right side down. Apply glue to cardboard. Press cardboard down on fabric at the center. Turn over and smooth out air bubbles and wrinkles. Turn back over. Apply glue to 1/2" outer edge of circle. Wrap excess fabric over edges, smoothing out as many wrinkles as possible.

# Painting

Before painting, wood should be prepared by sanding and sealing and should be free of dust and lint. Refer to instructions for Sanding to the right. Follow manufacturer's directions for sealing.

Using a flat paintbrush or, if preferred, a sponge brush, apply a smooth, even coat of acrylic paint. Allow to dry thoroughly.

If the wood grain raises, sand with fine-grit sandpaper or steel wool. If the grain is only slightly raised, a piece of brown paper sack can be used the same way fine-grit sandpaper is used. Wipe surfaces with a tack cloth to remove residue.

Apply a second coat of acrylic paint. Allow to dry thoroughly. If necessary, sand and paint again. Good coverage is generally achieved with two coats; however, some paint colors will require three coats.

When a very smooth surface is required, apply at least three coats of acrylic paint, using steel wool to sand between each coat. Make sure to remove residue by wiping surfaces with a tack cloth between coats.

# Preparing Boxes

Chipboard boxes are oftentimes referred to as chipwood boxes. They come in many sizes and shapes and are generally inexpensive.

The sides of these boxes are quite flimsy and must be reinforced to add strength. This can be done by simply placing a bead of hot glue around the inside bottom edge of the box (between the side and the bottom). Allow hot glue to harden.

Using an old paintbrush, apply a heavy layer of Tacky glue to the inside sides of the box. Allow to dry thoroughly.

Chipboard boxes usually have very smooth finishes; however, if there are any "bumps" on the outside, lightly sand with fine-grit sandpaper.

# Sanding

Items that will be painted or stained most always need to be sanded. Using medium-grit sandpaper, sand surfaces until smooth. Always sand in the direction of the natural wood grain to avoid cross-grain scratches. Continue sanding until all rough edges and scratches are removed. Shake dust off.

Repeat the process using fine-grit sandpaper. Surfaces should be smooth and free from rough edges. Make sure to remove residue by wiping surfaces with a tack cloth.

# Sculpting Clay Water

Place a piece of aluminum foil or plastic wrap on top of the box or basket. Knead the sculpting clay and press it on top of the box or basket in the desired shape and in an even layer.

Using the curved edge of a ceramic cleaning tool, push and lift clay to form "waves." Practice before actually sculpting the water for the music box.

When "waves" are sculpted, carefully remove clay from the aluminum foil or plastic wrap. Bake clay following manufacturer's directions. Allow to cool thoroughly.

## Staining

## Sponging

Dip a natural sponge into acrylic paint. Blot the sponge on a paper towel until there is only a very small amount of paint left on the sponge. Carefully press sponge onto the surface to be sponged and quickly lift it off to avoid smears. Continue sponging until desired areas are covered. Be careful not to go over the same area too many times or the area will become solid and look too heavy.

As the paint on the sponge is used and the sponging pattern starts to become too light, re-dip the sponge back into the acrylic paint. Repeat the process until desired areas are covered. Allow to dry thoroughly.

*Using wood stain:* There are many different types of wood stains available, as well as a vast number of stain colors. It is important to always follow manufacturer's directions. Stain can be applied with an old paintbrush or, if preferred, an old clean rag, a sponge brush, or steel wool.

All stains will stain differently, depending on the wood being used. The softness or hardness of the wood will determine how much stain is absorbed into the wood. The longer the stain is left on the wood, the darker the stain color will be. Stain can be wiped off after one or two minutes to achieve a light stain or left on for five or ten minutes to achieve a dark stain.

There are stains available that are combined with a wood sealer. These stains require a single coat and dry quickly; however, for these projects, it is recommended to use a stain that requires two to three coats. This will render a "richer" appearance. Make sure to sand with steel wool between each coat and wipe with a tack cloth.

Feel free to substitute any stain color for the stain color called for in the materials lists. Stain colors can be mixed to create new colors.

*Using acrylic paint:* Acrylic paint can be used as a staining medium by simply mixing it with water. Acrylic paint stain has the look of a colored stain. Start by mixing equal parts of acrylic paint and water in a plastic cup or bowl.

Using a paintbrush or, if preferred, a sponge brush, apply an even, consistent coat of acrylic paint stain over the entire surface. It is very important to apply stain evenly or an uneven color will appear. Allow to dry thoroughly.

Continue staining — do not stop and start. If the color is too light, re-mix stain using more acrylic paint. Stain entire surface again. Allow to dry thoroughly.

The wood grain will raise because of the water, but it is not necessary to sand the wood.

# Tea Dyeing

Tea dye can be purchased and used following manufacturer's directions, or tea dye can be home-made using a few tea bags.

Use a teacup for tea dyeing small items, such as lace and doilies. Use an old pot for tea dyeing larger items. Add boiling water to the teacup or old pot. Place tea bags in boiling water and allow to steep for

a few minutes. Check the color — when items are dry they appear a shade lighter. If color is too light after drying, items can be dyed again. If a darker color is desired, add more tea bags to the boiling water.

Immerse items for tea dyeing in teacup or old pot. When items are dyed the appropriate color, remove them from the teacup or old pot. Blot on paper towels — do not wring out. Allow to dry thoroughly, laying flat.

Tea dyeing can also be done by brushing the tea dye onto the item(s) to be dyed, such as a stuffed muslin animal. Prepare tea dye and, using a paint-brush or, if preferred, a sponge brush, apply an even amount to the entire surface. Allow to dry thoroughly.

# Transferring

When transferring patterns, begin by using a pencil to trace the pattern onto very thin, transparent tracing paper. After a neat tracing has been made, the design needs to be transferred to wood or fabric.

Position the pattern to be transferred on the wood or fabric. Place a sheet of graphite paper, graphite side down, under the sheet of tracing paper. Using a pencil or a stylus, carefully re-trace the pattern. When the tracing paper is removed, the pattern should be lightly, but neatly, transferred to the wood or fabric.

Homemade transfer paper can be made simply by using a pencil to re-trace the pattern on the back side of the tracing paper. Turn the tracing paper back over, position it on the wood or fabric, and carefully re-trace the pattern again.

It is important to remember that the finished painting can only be as good as the transferred design.

# Helpful Hints

## A Quick Way to Secure Musical Movements

When placing musical movements into music boxes, industrial-strength glue (or epoxy) is always used to secure them. When a musical movement is placed in a position where it can shift while the glue is drying, it is recommended that a few small dots of hot glue be placed at the edges of the musical movement to secure it until industrial-strength glue can dry thoroughly. Because hot glue dries quickly, an immediate bond is created, therefore the musical movement cannot shift out of position. Do not use a bead of hot glue all the way around the musical movement, as this will eliminate air flow, thus causing the industrial-strength glue to be unable to dry.

## Boxes with Pre-Drilled Holes

Boxes with pre-drilled holes can be purchased. They are usually called "musical memento boxes." Buying these boxes eliminates the drilling of the holes to accommodate the winding-key shafts and winding keys. However, when using a musical memento box, be sure to check the size of the hole with the accessories being used to make sure the fit is accurate.

## Outlining Made Simple

The trick to outlining is simple. Using a liner paintbrush, make sure paint is thinned with a small amount of water. Pull the paintbrush through the paint, rolling, to re-shape the bristles into a point. Be careful not to get the paint too thick.

## To Make Perfect Dots

When the need arises to paint decorative dots or "round" eyes and highlight dots, try using the end of a paintbrush (opposite the bristles). Different sizes of paintbrushes will render different sized dots. Practice with different sizes to get the desired size. If a larger dot is desired, the eraser on a new pencil works well. Dip the eraser or the end of the paintbrush into the paint each time a consistent sized dot is required.

## To Make Perfect Hearts

When the need arises to paint hearts, try using the end of a paintbrush (opposite the bristles). Make two "dots" next to each other so they touch slightly at the center. Using a small paintbrush, "pull" the paint down into a point or "V" and fill in the space with paint.

## Removing Mistakes When Detail Painting

If a mistake happens while detail painting, quickly use a baby wet wipe to wipe off the mistake. The wet wipe cleans the paint off before it absorbs into the base coat of paint. Remember to keep them within reach.

## Sealing Hard to Coat Surfaces

If the box being used for a particular music box has a hard to coat surface, such as paint, and refinishing the box is not desired, acrylic primer/sealer can be used. This sealer is painted on as a base coat and any paint will adhere to it. This sealer has a white finish, but colored paint can be added to the sealer so the base coat can actually be the desired color.

# Carousel Waltz

## Materials Needed

### For the Base, Including Music Box Accessories:
Round chipboard box, 2" high x 4$\frac{1}{2}$" diameter
Round wooden plaque, 4" diameter x $\frac{1}{4}$" thick
18-note key-wind musical movement
Top-mount rotation assembly
Left-hand threaded turntable, 2$\frac{1}{2}$"
T-bar winding key, $\frac{3}{4}$"
4 wooden knobs, 1"
Sandpaper
Wood sealer

### Decorative Accessories for Music Box Pictured:
3 resin carousel horses, 3$\frac{1}{4}$"

### Acrylic Paint Colors and Antiquing Gel:
Black
Cream
Dark blue
Dark brown
Dark gray
Dark green
Dark purple
Dark yellow
Light blue
Light brown
Light gray
Light purple
Mctallic gold
Plum
Raspberry
Rose
Brown antiquing gel

### Adhesives and Spray Sealer:
Hot glue sticks
Industrial-strength glue
Tacky glue
Gloss spray sealer

### Tools and Brushes:
Drill with $\frac{1}{4}$" and $\frac{1}{2}$" drill bits
Glue gun
Old clean rag
Old paintbrushes
Paintbrushes

*Floral Pattern*

## Step-by-Step Assembly

### Step One:
Prepare chipboard box. Refer to instructions for Preparing Boxes on page 14.

### Step Two:
Using sandpaper, sand plaque. Refer to instructions for Sanding on page 14. Using an old paintbrush, apply wood sealer to plaque and box following manufacturer's directions. Allow to dry thoroughly.

### Step Three:
Using a paintbrush, paint box base with rose acrylic paint and lid with light gray. Paint plaque with raspberry. Paint knobs with plum. Refer to instructions for Painting on page 14.

### Step Four:
Transfer floral pattern at left to side of lid. Refer to instructions for Transferring on page 16. Paint outlining with black. Mix plum with equal parts of water and paint flowers. Mix dark green with equal parts of water and paint leaves. Using the end of a small paintbrush, paint dots around vines with dark green. Dot metallic gold in center of flowers.

### Step Five:
Spray wood pieces with a light coat of gloss sealer — this prevents too much of the antiquing gel from absorbing into paint. Allow to dry thoroughly.

### Step Six:
Base-paint carousel horses with two coats of cream acrylic paint, letting each coat dry beforc applying the next. Paint mane and tail of one horse with dark brown, one horse with light brown, and one horse with light gray. Paint all hooves with dark gray. Paint saddles, bridles, and flowers with paint, referring to photograph for paint colors or paint as desired. Dot eyes with black. Paint poles and bases with two coats of metallic gold, letting each coat dry before applying the next.

### Step Seven:
Using an old paintbrush, antique carousel horses, plaque, box, and knobs with brown antiquing gel.

Refer to instructions for Antiquing on page 12. Spray all pieces with gloss sealer.

### Step Eight:

Drill a ¹/₂" hole in center top of lid. Using industrial-strength glue, glue left-hand threaded turntable to center bottom of plaque.

### Step Nine:

Attach top-mount rotation assembly to musical movement following manufacturer's directions. Referring to diagram below, place musical movement inside box. Place lid on top, making sure top-mount rotation assembly shaft is centered in hole. Remove the lid. Draw a line around musical movement. Remove musical movement and paint a small dot of paint on the bottom of the winding-key shaft. Press musical movement back into box so dot of paint marks placement for hole and remove once hole has been marked. Drill a ¹/₄" hole using paint dot as the center mark. Using industrial-strength glue, glue musical movement into box, making sure winding-key shaft is centered in hole. Glue knobs, evenly spaced, to bottom of box for legs. Allow to dry thoroughly.

### Step Ten:

Using Tacky glue, glue lid on box. Wind left-hand threaded turntable onto top-mount rotation assembly. Using industrial-strength glue, glue carousel horses, evenly spaced, to top of plaque ¹/₄" from edge. Wind on winding key. Wind musical movement so music is playing to be sure horses are facing the right direction. Allow to dry thoroughly.

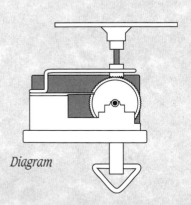

*Diagram*

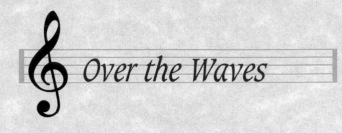
## Materials Needed

### For the Base, Including Music Box Accessories:
Round chipboard box, 1³/₄" high x 4" diameter
Round wooden plaque, 3¹/₂" diameter x ³/₄" thick
Balsa wood, 3" x 3" x ¹/₄" thick
18-note key-wind musical movement
Turntable, 2¹/₂"
4 wooden beads, ³/₄"
Sandpaper
Wood sealer

### Decorative Accessories for Music Box Pictured:
Resin carousel horse, 3¹/₄"

### Acrylic Paint Colors and Antiquing Gel:
Black
Dark gray
Light gray
Metallic gold
Pastel blue
Pastel lavender
Pastel peach
Pastel pink
Pastel turquoise
Pastel yellow
Black antiquing gel

### Adhesives and Spray Sealer:
Hot glue sticks
Industrial-strength glue
Tacky glue
Gloss spray sealer

*Zig-zag Pattern*

*Continued on page 22.*

# *Over the Waves*

Continued from page 20.

## Tools and Brushes:

Drill with $1/2$" drill bit
Glue gun
Old clean rag
Old paintbrushes
Paintbrushes

# Step-by-Step Assembly

### Step One:

Prepare chipboard box. Refer to instructions for Preparing Boxes on page 14.

### Step Two:

Using sandpaper, sand plaque. Refer to instructions for Sanding on page 14. Using industrial-strength glue, glue balsa wood to inside center of lid. Using an old paintbrush, apply wood sealer to plaque and box following manufacturer's directions. Allow to dry thoroughly.

### Step Three:

Using a paintbrush, paint box base with pastel pink acrylic paint and lid with pastel turquoise. Paint plaque with pastel lavender and edge around plaque with pastel yellow. Paint beads with metallic gold. Refer to photograph. Refer to instructions for Painting on page 14.

### Step Four:

Transfer zig-zag pattern from page 20 to side of lid. Refer to instructions for Transferring on page 16. Paint with metallic gold, pastel peach, and pastel blue. Using the end of a medium paintbrush, paint peach dots. Allow to dry thoroughly. Using the end of a small paintbrush, paint blue dots on top of peach dots.

### Step Five:

Spray wood pieces with a light coat of gloss sealer — this prevents too much of the antiquing gel from absorbing into paint. Allow to dry thoroughly.

### Step Six:

Base-paint carousel horse with two coats of light gray acrylic paint, letting each coat dry before applying the next. Paint mane, tail, and hooves with dark gray. Paint saddle, bridle, flowers, and leaves with pastel paints, referring to photograph for paint colors or paint as desired. Dot eyes with black. Paint pole and base with two coats of metallic gold, letting each coat dry before applying the next.

### Step Seven:

Using an old paintbrush, antique carousel horse, plaque, box, and beads with black antiquing gel. Refer to instructions for Antiquing on page 12. Spray all pieces with gloss sealer.

### Step Eight:

Drill a $1/2$" hole in center top of lid. Using industrial-strength glue, glue turntable to center bottom of plaque. Glue musical movement to inside of lid on balsa wood, making sure winding-key shaft is centered in hole. Glue beads, evenly spaced, to bottom of box for legs. Allow to dry thoroughly.

### Step Nine:

Using Tacky glue, glue lid on box. Wind turntable onto musical movement. Using industrial-strength glue, glue carousel horse to center of plaque. The turntable is the winding key. Allow to dry thoroughly.

# Music Box Variation

Because this is a basic and simple music box, using the turntable as the winding key, it would be easy to change the carousel horse on top to anything desired.

- Try a dancing ballerina with the box painted with feminine colors. The border around the lid could be a pattern of musical notes or flowing ribbons.

# *Let Me Call You Sweetheart*

## Materials Needed

### For the Base, Including Music Box Accessories:
Round printed tin, 2" high x 5½" diameter
18-note key-wind musical movement
Key extender, ½"
T-bar winding key, ¾"
Découpage

### Decorative Accessories for Music Box Pictured:
Ceramic cherub, 4"
3 filigree leaf charms, 1"
2 pearl beads
White crocheted doily, 6" round
1½"-wide red crocheted lace, ¾ yard
½"-wide light gray silk ribbon, 16"
½"-wide dark gray silk ribbon, 1 yard
4mm mauve silk ribbon, 5"
7mm mauve silk ribbon, ½ yard
7mm blue silk ribbon, ½ yard
1"-wide dark green silk ribbon, 20"
Matching thread for lace and ribbons

### Acrylic Paint Color and Antiquing Gel:
Metallic gold
Black antiquing gel

### Adhesives and Spray Sealer:
Hot glue sticks
Industrial-strength glue
Gloss spray sealer

### Tools and Brushes:
Dressmaker's pen
Drill with ¼" drill bit
Glue gun
Needle
Old clean rag
Old paintbrushes
Paintbrush
Scissors

## Step-by-Step Assembly

### Step One:
Drill a ¼" hole at center back of tin ¾" from bottom. If tin is rounded, a key extender is necessary. Wind key extender onto musical movement. Place musical movement inside tin. Wind winding key onto key extender from the outside, making sure winding-key shaft is centered in hole.

### Step Two:
Using industrial-strength glue, glue musical movement inside tin. Glue lid on tin.

### Step Three:
Using an old paintbrush, apply a thin layer of découpage to top of lid. Centering doily, press it on top and over edges of lid. Apply a moderate coat of découpage over doily. Refer to instructions for Découpaging on page 12.

### Step Four:
Using red crocheted lace, make one lace rose. Using light gray silk ribbon, make two violets. Using dark gray silk ribbon, make three rosettes. Using mauve silk ribbons, make three rosettes. Using blue silk ribbon, make two rosettes. Using dark green silk ribbon, make five ribbon petals. Refer to instructions and diagrams on page 25.

### Step Five:
Using a paintbrush, paint cherub with metallic gold acrylic paint. Refer to instructions for Painting on page 14.

### Step Six:
Using an old paintbrush, antique cherub and filigree leaf charms with black antiquing gel. Refer to instructions for Antiquing on page 12. Spray all pieces with gloss sealer.

### Step Seven:
Using industrial-strength glue, glue cherub on top of lid. Refer to photograph. Allow to dry thoroughly.

### Step Eight:
Using a glue gun, hot-glue flowers, petals, and filigree leaf charms to top of lid, referring to photograph. One violet and two leaves are at back of lace rose to cover stitches. Glue one pearl bead to each violet center.

## Lace Rose:

Fold ends of lace at right angles. Stitch running thread on long, straight raw edge, leaving needle and thread attached.

Gather lace slightly, simultaneously wrapping to make a rose. Force needle through lower lace edge and secure thread. Trim excess lace below stitches and fluff flower.

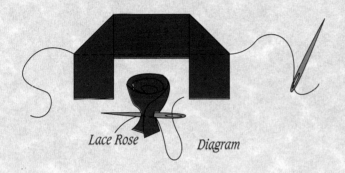

*Lace Rose*   *Diagram*

## Violet:

Cut ribbon into 8" lengths. Using dressmaker's pen, mark ¹/₂" allowance on each end of ribbon. Measure and mark scallop length from first mark 1¹/₄" apart. Stitch running thread as shown and gather tightly. Stitch short ends, forming a circle. Wrap thread around stitches to secure. Trim excess ribbon below stitches and fluff flower.

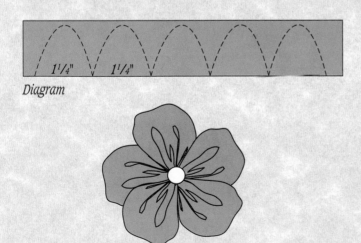

1¹/₄"   1¹/₄"

*Diagram*

*Violet*

## Rosette:

For 4mm ribbon rosettes, cut 5" ribbon lengths. For 7mm ribbon rosettes, cut 9" ribbon lengths. For ¹/₂" ribbon rosettes, cut 12" ribbon lengths. Mark center of ribbon lengths. Beginning at one end, fold end forward at a right angle. Holding vertical length, begin rolling ribbon at fold horizontally to form bud.

Then, fold horizontal ribbon backward at right angle and continue rolling bud, aligning top edges of bud to second fold (rounding corner).

Continue folding ribbon backward at right angles and rolling bud to center mark. Secure, leaving needle and thread attached.

Stitch running thread on edge of remaining ribbon length and gather tightly. Wrap gathered ribbon around bud. Secure and fluff flower.

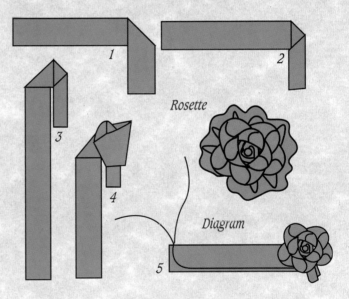

1   2   3   4   5

*Rosette*

*Diagram*

## Ribbon Petal:

Cut ribbon into 4" lengths. Fold ribbon into thirds, overlapping sides. Stitch running thread. Gather tightly and wrap thread around stitches to secure. Trim excess ribbon and fluff petal.

*Diagram*   *Ribbon Petal*

# *Love Story*

## Materials Needed

### For the Base, Including Music Box Accessories:
Heart-shaped blue and burgundy sewing basket,
  5$^1/_2$" high x 31" circumference
Hardboard circle, 6" diameter x $^1/_8$" thick
18-note key-wind miniature musical movement
Miniature turntable, 3"

### Decorative Accessories for Music Box Pictured:
2 wooden thimbles, 1"
8 wooden thread spools, (3) $^1/_2$", (5) 1"
Blue velvet, 8$^1/_2$" circle
Burgundy embroidery floss
Country-blue embroidery floss
Ecru embroidery floss
Gray embroidery floss
Green embroidery floss
Rose embroidery floss
$^3/_8$"-wide ecru flat lace, 10"
Small rose flat braid trim, 7"
4mm light pink silk ribbon, 17"
4mm rose silk ribbon, 12"
Heavyweight cardboard, 4" x 5"
Lightweight rose fabric, 6" x 9"
Small ball of blue tatting thread
Small ball of ecru tatting thread
Small ball of rose tatting thread
Stuffing
$^7/_8$"-wide burgundy and gold
  wire-edged ribbon, 1$^1/_4$ yards
Ecru doily, 8" round
Silver heart button, $^3/_4$"
Sewing machine (pencil sharpener),
  2$^1/_2$" wide x 2$^1/_4$" high
Skein of dark blue wool
Skein of rose wool
Brass "stork" scissors, 4"
Straight pins
Needle threader
2 needles
Brass thimble, $^3/_4$"
2 silver thimbles, $^3/_4$"
Assortment of buttons, $^3/_4$"

Strong blue thread to match blue velvet
Rose thread to match rose fabric
Tea dye or tea bags

### Stain:
Medium walnut stain

### Adhesives and Spray Sealer:
Hot glue sticks
Industrial-strength glue
Tacky glue, thin-bodied
Matte spray sealer

### Tools and Brushes:
Glue gun
Needle
Old clean rag
Old paintbrushes
Paintbrush
Paper towels
Scissors
Sewing machine
X-acto knife or razor blade

## Step-by-Step Assembly

### Step One:
Using an old paintbrush, stain wooden thimbles and thread spools. Refer to instructions for Staining on pages 15-16. Spray with matte sealer.

### Step Two:
Using scissors, cut a 2" cross (+) in the top center of sewing basket lid. Remove enough stuffing or foam so musical movement will sit on hard surface inside. Using industrial-strength glue, glue miniature musical movement to the hard surface, winding-key shaft pointing up. Place a small amount of thin-bodied Tacky glue on the cut edges of fabric to prevent fraying. Allow to dry thoroughly.

### Step Three:
Using matching thread, fold edges of blue velvet circle under $^1/_4$". Hand-sew a gathering stitch $^1/_8$" from edge. Lay velvet circle right side down. Using an old paintbrush, apply a thin layer of thin-bodied Tacky

glue to hardboard circle. Centering, place glue side down onto velvet. Pull gathers tightly. Tie a few knots and trim ends. Using industrial-strength glue, glue miniature turntable to center bottom of hardboard circle, shaft side up. Allow to dry thoroughly.

### Step Four:

Wrap thread spools with embroidery floss, leaving 3" to 4" tails. Blue and burgundy embroidery floss get used twice. Using an X-acto knife or razor blade, cut a small "slit" in the top edge of each spool so the embroidery floss can be secured on spool (similar to purchased thread spools).

### Step Five:

Tea-dye doily, $3/8$"-wide lace, braid trim, silk ribbons, and lightweight rose fabric. Using a paint-brush, brush tea dye on embroidery floss and balls

of tatting thread. Refer to instructions for Tea Dyeing on page 16.

### Step Six:

If musical movement is higher than basket top, add more stuffing to lid top, under fabric. Tie a bow in center of wire-edged ribbon. Using a glue gun, hot-glue bow to top of basket 1" from the "V" on the heart. Cascade ribbons around edges of basket by twisting ribbon tightly every few inches and turning ribbon. Hot-glue ribbon to top of basket at the tight twist points. Continue to ends of ribbon. Trim ends on an angle. Refer to photograph.

### Step Seven:

Wind miniature turntable onto musical movement. Using an old paintbrush, apply a thin layer of thin-bodied Tacky glue to back of doily. Do not apply to

28

outer 1" edge. Centering, press doily onto velvet circle. Allow to dry thoroughly.

### Step Eight:

To make pincushion, use the patterns at right. Using scissors, cut large and small ovals from heavy-weight cardboard. To make pincushion base, cut one rose fabric oval ½" larger than large cardboard oval. Lay fabric, right side down, and center large cardboard oval on fabric. Wrap fabric over and, using a glue gun, hot-glue around the edges, smoothing wrinkles.

### Step Nine:

Cut a 2¼" x 8½" strip from rose fabric. Using a sewing machine, sew, right sides together, a ¼" seam allowance along 2¼" edge. Turn right side out. Place small cardboard oval inside fabric "tube." Hot-glue ½" to bottom of cardboard. Fold top edge under ¼". Hand-sew a gathering stitch ⅛" from edge. Lightly fill with stuffing and pull threads to gather. Adjust gathers and stitch closed. Before cutting threads, sew ¾" silver heart button to center of pincushion.

### Step Ten:

Cut 5" of light pink silk ribbon. Make one ribbon rosette. Refer to instructions and diagram on page 25. Handling light pink and rose silk ribbon as one, tie a small bow at center. Tie a knot in each set of ribbon tails 2" from bow. Hot-glue bow to side of silver heart button. Hot-glue knots to pincushion, leaving ribbon very loose and "loopy." Loosely wrap ends of tails under pincushion and hot-glue in place. Attach braid trim the same way, but do not tie a bow. Hot-glue ribbon rosette on top of bow center. Hot-glue ⅜"-wide lace around bottom edge of pincushion. Centering, glue pincushion to pincushion base. Refer to photograph.

### Step Eleven:

Using industrial-strength glue, glue all decorative accessories to top of doily. The turntable is the winding key. Stick a few straight pins in pincushion and thread needles onto two spools of floss. Stick needles in spools. Glue floss tails down. Allow to dry thoroughly. Refer to photograph on page 28.

2¼"    3¼"    2"    3"

*Pincushion Patterns — Enlarge 135%*

*If preferred, try a pincushion with a different shape — maybe a heart or a circle. Enlarge 135%*

# *Try to Remember*

## Materials Needed

### For the Base, Including Music Box Accessories:

Double recipe box,
   $7\frac{1}{2}$" wide x $5\frac{3}{4}$" deep x $3\frac{3}{4}$" high
Hardboard, $6\frac{3}{8}$" x 4" x $\frac{1}{2}$" thick
3 squares of balsa wood, $1\frac{7}{8}$" x $1\frac{7}{8}$" x $\frac{1}{4}$" thick
18-note key-wind musical movement
Triangle ring winding key, $\frac{3}{4}$"

### Decorative Accessories for Music Box Pictured:

Peel-n-stick floral-print fabric, 5.63-sq.-ft. roll
1 gold stick pin, 7"
1 silver stick pin, 7"
4 small beads or pearls
Gold heart pendant
Silver baroque pendant
4mm green silk ribbon, 20"
4mm peach silk ribbon, 20"
4 brass corner brackets, $1\frac{1}{2}$"
Gold-tone chain, 5"
2 small brass eye hooks
Oval mirror, 4" high x $3\frac{1}{4}$" wide
$\frac{3}{8}$"-wide green flat braided trim, 12"
Scraps of old lace
Oval silver-plated easel-backed photo frame,
   $2\frac{1}{2}$" wide x $3\frac{3}{4}$" high
Cold-cream jar, 3" wide x $2\frac{1}{2}$" high
Perfume bottle, $2\frac{1}{4}$" high
Lipstick tube and case
Pair of women's gloves
Pair of brass doll glasses, $3\frac{1}{2}$"
Miniature Bible, $1\frac{1}{4}$"
Assortment of jewelry:
   pearl necklaces, brooches, earrings, rings, etc.
Tea dye or tea bags

### Acrylic Enamel Paint:

White gloss acrylic enamel

### Adhesives:

Hot glue sticks
Industrial-strength glue
Super glue
Tacky glue

### Tools and Brushes:

Drill with $\frac{1}{4}$" drill bit
Glue gun
Hammer
Paintbrush
Paper towels
Rotary cutter
Ruler

## Step-by-Step Assembly

### Step One:

Using a ruler and rotary cutter, cut peel-n-stick floral-print fabric as follows: $13\frac{1}{2}$" x $11\frac{3}{4}$" piece for lid, 7" x $5\frac{1}{4}$" piece for inside lid, $27\frac{1}{4}$" x 5" piece for bottom sides, $7\frac{1}{4}$" x $5\frac{5}{8}$" piece for bottom, and $6\frac{7}{8}$" x $5\frac{1}{8}$" piece for hardboard.

### Step Two:

Remove the wooden center divider from inside recipe box. Cover box and hardboard with peel-n-stick fabric following manufacturer's directions. Apply fabric to lid first, centering on top; miter and trim corners, wrapping around sides to the inside of lid. Apply fabric to inside lid. Apply fabric piece to bottom sides, wrapping $\frac{1}{4}$" to box bottom; miter and trim top corners, wrapping to the inside box. Apply fabric to bottom. Apply remaining fabric to hardboard. Using a small amount of Tacky glue, glue corners down if they are pulling up.

### Step Three:

Drill a $\frac{1}{4}$" hole in box back $\frac{3}{4}$" from bottom, centering hole from side to side. Using industrial-strength glue, glue musical movement to inside of box, making sure winding-key shaft is centered in hole. The long side of musical movement must be horizontal so it is $1\frac{7}{8}$" high. Glue squares of balsa wood inside box. Glue one piece to each side of box, centering from side to side, with bottom edge touching bottom of box. The hardboard will rest on these squares and the musical movement. Allow to dry thoroughly.

**Step Four:**

Wash and dry the inside of cold-cream jar. With a paintbrush, paint the inside with white gloss acrylic enamel. Allow to dry thoroughly and put lid on jar.

**Step Five:**

Tea-dye women's gloves and silk ribbon. Refer to instructions for Tea Dyeing on page 16.

**Step Six:**

To make fancy hat pins, start with stick pins. Slide one pearl or bead on-to silver stick pin. Slide silver baroque pendant on next. The peach silk ribbon goes on next. Turn ribbon under $1/4$" and stick the stick pin through the ribbon at center. Spacing 1", stick the stick pin back through. Do not twist ribbon. Continue until the ribbon is completely threaded onto the stick pin. At the end of the ribbon, fold under $1/4$" and stick the stick pin through very close to the fold. Push ribbon "loops" to the top of the stick pin, just below silver baroque pendant, so they are tight. Fluff ribbon "loops." Using super glue, apply a small amount on the stick pin next to ribbon and slide on one pearl or bead. Refer to diagram at right. Allow to dry thoroughly. Repeat process to make another fancy hat pin, using gold heart pendant and green silk ribbon.

*Fancy Hat Pin Diagram*

**Step Seven:**

Carefully hammer corner brackets on top corners of box.

**Step Eight:**

Using industrial-strength glue, glue hardboard in box, resting on balsa wood and musical movement. Attach chain from lid to chest on left-hand side using eye hooks. Apply a small amount of super glue to hinges so lid cannot close. Using industrial-strength glue, glue oval mirror to inside center of lid. Allow to dry thoroughly.

**Step Nine:**

Using a glue gun, hot-glue flat braided trim around mirror. Hot-glue scraps of old lace around sides and back of box. Refer to photograph.

**Step Ten:**

Arrange decorative accessories inside box. Refer to photograph. When items are inside box, according to photograph or placed as desired, glue in place using industrial-strength glue. Allow to dry thoroughly. Wind on winding key.

## Music Box Variations

- This would be the perfect music box to make and give as a special gift. One idea would be to fill the music box with treasured trinkets and mementos, such as items that have been passed down through the generations. Any of grandma's jewelry, bottles, cosmetic compacts, etc. would add interest and timelessness to the music box. Wouldn't a mother appreciate a gift such as this, filled with her mother's belongings and knick-knacks?

- A box covered with fabric, inside and out, could be used as a "Planter Box" music box. Using supplies for making a floral arrangement (floral foam, Spanish moss, and floral pins) arrange a "dried" or "silk" floral arrangement in the box. Use an 18-note key wind musical movement placed in the back of the box. The musical movement can be covered with the Spanish moss by simply using Tacky glue to glue it to the musical movement. A beautiful bow, made from wire-edged crinkled satin ribbon or craft ribbon, would be a nice accent to the floral arrangement. If desired, wooden beads or candle cups can be stained or painted and, using industrial strength glue, glued to the bottom corners for legs.

# *Easter Parade*

## Materials Needed

### For the Base, Including Music Box Accessories:
Round heavy-duty wooden basket,
    11" high (including handle) x 8" diameter
Hardboard, 9" x 9" x $1/4$" thick
18-note key-wind musical movement
Turntable, 3"
Textured snow
Sandpaper
Wood sealer

### Decorative Accessories for Music Box Pictured:
Prepainted figurines (resin, porcelain, or wooden):
    3 gardening rabbits
    3 small rabbits
    House
    Tree
    Truck
2"-wide light blue wire-edged
    crinkled satin ribbon, $1^3/4$ yards

### Acrylic Paint Colors:
Green to match grass on figurines
Light green
Pink

### Adhesives and Spray Sealer:
Hot glue sticks
Industrial-strength glue
Gloss spray sealer

### Tools and Brushes:
Drill with $1/4$" drill bit
Glue gun
Old paintbrushes
Paintbrush
Paper towels
Ruler
Saw

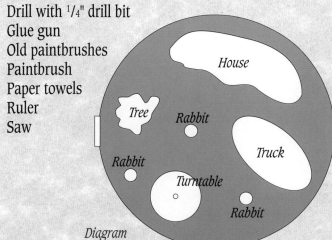

Diagram

## Step-by-Step Assembly

### Step One:
Using a ruler, measure diameter of basket across the top to get an exact measurement. Using that measurement, draw a circle on hardboard. Using a saw, cut circle out.

### Step Two:
Drill a $1/4$" hole $1^3/4$" from edge of circle to accommodate winding-key shaft.

### Step Three:
Using an old paintbrush, apply textured snow to top and sides of hardboard circle and to top of turntable following manufacturer's directions. Allow to dry thoroughly.

### Step Four:
If necessary, use sandpaper to sand basket. Refer to instructions for Sanding on page 14. Using an old paintbrush, apply wood sealer to basket following manufacturer's directions. Allow to dry thoroughly.

### Step Five:
Using a paintbrush, paint sealed basket with pink acrylic paint. Refer to instructions for Painting on page 14. Spray with gloss sealer.

### Step Six:
Paint textured snow with two coats of green. Allow to dry thoroughly. Dry-brush over painted textured snow with light green. Refer to instructions for Dry Brushing on page 13. Spray with gloss sealer.

### Step Seven:
Using industrial-strength glue, glue musical movement to bottom side of hardboard circle, making sure winding-key shaft is centered in hole. Allow to dry thoroughly.

### Step Eight:
Glue hardboard circle to basket top. Refer to diagram at left for placement of hole for turntable. Allow to dry thoroughly.

Using industrial-strength glue, glue figurines to top of hardboard circle. Wind turntable onto musical movement. Glue gardening rabbits on top of turntable. The turntable is the winding key. Refer to diagram on page 34 for placement.

### Step Ten:

Using the wire-edged ribbon, tie a bow in the center. Using a glue gun, hot-glue bow 2" to the left of center on basket handle. Cascade ribbon down basket handle and on the basket front by twisting ribbon tightly every $3^1/2$" to 4" and turning ribbon. Hot-glue ribbon at the tight twist points. Refer to photograph.

# Music Box Variations

- It is simple to turn this music box into one that anyone with "western flair" would love. Instead of applying textured snow to hardboard circle, glue "hay" onto the hardboard circle using Tacky glue. Decorate the top of the hay-covered hardboard circle with western charms and miniatures. Refer to "Country Roads" on page 68 for a list of materials needed. The basket can be stained instead of being painted.

- It is simple to turn this music box into a "memory" box. Instead of applying textured snow to hardboard circle, paint it with acrylic paint. Refer to instructions for Painting on page 14. Using Tacky glue, glue a tea-dyed doily onto painted hardboard circle. Refer to instructions for Tea Dyeing on page 16. Using industrial-strength glue, any item with sentimental value can be glued to the top of the doily. For instance, try a teacup and teaspoon, an assortment of grandma's costume jewelry or her spectacles, or maybe baby's first pair of shoes or first hair brush and mirror set.

- It is simple to turn this music box into one appropriate for a baby shower gift. Instead of applying textured snow to hardboard circle, paint it with acrylic paint. Refer to instructions for Painting on page 14. Using industrial-strength glue, glue miscellaneous baby items to the top of the painted hardboard circle. Do not glue the plywood circle to the basket — use it as a lid. Fill the inside of the basket with several baby items, such as baby lotion, baby shampoo, Q-tips, cotton balls, pacifiers, nail clippers, bibs, bonnets, baby spoons, etc. Any craft ribbon would work well for the bow.

- It is simple to turn this music box into one appropriate for holiday gift-giving. Using industrial-strength glue, glue prepainted wooden nutcrackers to the top of the unpainted textured snow. Do not glue the hardboard circle to the basket — use it as a lid. Fill the inside of the basket with mixed nuts.

- It is simple to turn this music box into a "trick-or-treat" basket. Paint the surface of the textured snow with black or orange acrylic paint. Using industrial-strength glue, glue miscellaneous Halloween figurines to the top of the painted textured snow. Do not glue the hardboard circle to the basket — use it as a lid. Fill the inside of the basket with candy.

- It is simple to turn this music box into a bread basket. Stain the basket and the hardboard instead of painting them. The plywood must be a good quality grade. Refer to instructions for Staining on pages 15-16. Allow croissants, breadsticks, a miniature loaf of bread, and crackers to dry out until hard. Using an old paintbrush, apply a moderate layer of découpage to entire surfaces. Allow to dry thoroughly. Using industrial-strength glue, glue to the top of the stained lid. Place a scarf into the basket and fill with an assortment of dinner rolls or crackers.

## Materials Needed

### For the Base, Including Music Box Accessories:
Round chipboard box, 2¼" high x 5" diameter
Square of wood, 2½" x 2½" x ½" thick
18-note key-wind musical movement,
  including magnetic swing arm
Key extender, ⅜"
T-bar winding key, ¾"
4 wooden beads, ½"

### Decorative Accessories for Music Box Pictured:
3 prepainted resin bunny figurines, 2"
Prepainted resin Easter tree, 3½"
Round beveled mirror, 5" diameter
5"-wide floral-print net ribbon, 24"
½"-wide pink braided trim, 16"

### Acrylic Paint Colors:
Ivory
Medium pink

### Adhesives and Spray Sealer:
Hot glue sticks
Industrial-strength glue
Tacky glue
Tacky glue, thin-bodied
Matte spray sealer

### Tools and Brushes:
Drill with ¼" drill bit
Glue gun
Old paintbrush
Paintbrush
Scissors

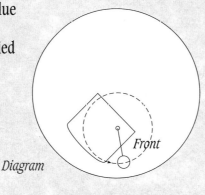

Diagram

## Step-by-Step Assembly

### Step One:
Prepare chipboard box. Refer to instructions for Preparing Boxes on page 14.

### Step Two:
Using a paintbrush, paint box and lid with ivory acrylic paint. Paint beads with medium pink. Refer to instructions for Painting on page 14. Spray with matte sealer.

### Step Three:
Cut one strip from net ribbon, 15¾" x 2¾", and one 4½" circle. Using thin-bodied Tacky glue, laminate net ribbon strip to side of box, lining up top edge. Cut small notches in ½" overhang, laminating to box bottom and making sure it is flat and smooth. Centering, laminate 4½" circle to box bottom. Refer to instructions for Laminating on page 13.

### Step Four:
Using industrial-strength glue, glue square of wood to inside center front of box bottom to which musical movement will be glued. Allow to dry thoroughly.

### Step Five:
To mark the hole position for winding-key shaft, place musical movement inside box at front center (seam is at back). Refer to diagram at left. Draw a line around musical movement. Remove musical movement and place a dot of paint on winding-key shaft. Press musical movement, winding-key shaft side down, back in box. Remove musical movement and drill a ¼" hole in box, centering on paint dot.

### Step Six:
Using industrial-strength glue, glue beads, evenly spaced, to bottom of box for legs. Glue musical movement into box, centering winding-key shaft in hole.

### Step Seven:
Using Tacky glue, glue lid on box. Glue braided trim to side of lid. Using industrial-strength glue, glue mirror to top of lid. Glue the magnet that comes with musical movement to bottom of bunny that has been chosen to dance and twirl. Allow to dry thoroughly.

### Step Eight:
Wind key extender onto winding key. Wind key extender onto winding-key shaft so music is playing. Place bunny with magnet on top of mirror. Place tree at center back of box and remaining bunnies on each side of tree. Refer to photograph for placement. Move tree and bunnies as needed so dancing bunny does not bump into them. When they are positioned correctly, glue on with a small amount of industrial-strength glue. Be careful that excess glue does not seep out from under figurines so it does not show on the mirror.

# *Raindrops Keep Falling*

## Materials Needed

### For the Base, Including Music Box Accessories:

5-piece metal garden set:
- Watering can, 8" high (including handle) x $5^1/2$" diameter
- Flower mister
- Shovel, rake, and hoe

18-note key-wind double-action musical movement

T-bar winding key, $^3/4$"

4 wooden beads, $^3/4$"

Découpage

Sandpaper

### Decorative Accessories for Music Box Pictured:

6 stickers of seed packets, $1^1/2$" x 2"

Wooden plug, 1"

Wooden egg half, $1^1/4$"

4 wooden hearts, (2) 1", (2) $1^1/2$"

Wooden candle cup, $1^1/2$"

Wooden dowel, $^5/16$" diameter x $1^5/8$" length

3 wooden dowels, $^3/16$" diameter x $1^1/4$" lengths

6 small straight pins

Small silk sunflowers

Gold cording, 4 yards

18-gauge wire, 15"

Tea dye or tea bags

### Acrylic Paint Colors and Acrylic Enamel Paint:

Black

Green to match watering can color

Off-white

Orange

Red

White

Yellow

Black gloss acrylic enamel

### Adhesives and Spray Sealer:

Hot glue sticks

Industrial-strength glue

Super glue

Gloss spray sealer

### Tools and Brushes:

Drill with $^1/4$", $^1/16$", and $^3/32$" drill bits

Glue gun

Hammer

Old paintbrush

Paintbrush

Paper towels

Saw

Scissors

Screwdriver

Wire cutters

## Step-by-Step Assembly

### Step One:

Remove backing from stickers, and place them on watering can and flower mister. Four stickers go on watering can and two stickers go on flower mister. Using an old paintbrush, apply a thin layer of découpage over stickers — carefully go over all edges to make sure they are sealed. Refer to instructions for Découpaging on page 12.

### Step Two:

Tea-dye sunflowers. Refer to instructions for Tea Dyeing on page 16.

### Step Three:

Using a paintbrush, paint beads with acrylic paint to match watering can color (green). Paint plug with red, the egg half with yellow, the 1" hearts with off-white, and the $1^1/2$" hearts with orange. Refer to instructions for Painting on page 14.

### Step Four:

Using a saw, cut points off the orange hearts at a 20° angle. Paint details on ladybug, butterfly, and bumblebee. Refer to patterns on page 40 for paint colors. Using sandpaper, round off ends of the $^5/16$" dowel to make butterfly body. Paint with black. Carefully hammer small straight pins in for antennae. Paint straight pins with black gloss acrylic enamel.

### Step Five:

Using industrial-strength glue, glue wings onto bumblebee and butterfly bodies. Allow to dry thoroughly. Spray bugs and beads with gloss sealer.

### Step Six:

Glue candle cup to center top of turntable on double-action musical movement. Allow to dry thoroughly. Drill holes in center bottom of watering can using the template below. Place musical movement inside watering can. Using wire cutters, trim flower stems so flowers come just above top edge of watering can when glued inside candle cup. Remove musical movement from watering can. Using a glue gun, hot-glue flowers into cup. Using industrial-strength glue, glue beads, evenly spaced, to bottom of watering can for legs. Allow to dry thoroughly.

### Step Seven:

Drill a $1/16$" hole into one end of each of the $3/16$" dowels. Using wire cutters, cut 18-gauge wire into three 5" lengths. Using super glue, glue the wire lengths into dowels. Drill a $3/32$" hole into the other end of dowels. Holding musical movement upside down, glue dowels to small disks on top of turntable. It is important to do this upside down to prevent the glue from dripping onto oscillating rods.

### Step Eight:

Place musical movement into watering can and secure it with screws following manufacturer's directions. Wind on winding key.

### Step Nine:

Drill a $1/16$" hole into bottom center of each bug. Using wire cutters, trim 18-gauge wires so the bugs are at different levels — this prevents them from bumping into each other. Place bugs on stems. Wind musical movement and make sure everything is moving properly and nothing is bumping. Using super glue, glue bugs on 18-gauge wire stems.

### Step Ten:

Using scissors, cut gold cording in half. With the first 2-yard length, tie a knot 1" from both ends. Loop back and forth around fingers to make a bow. Tie bow to watering can handle with a small piece of cording

and tie a knot 1" from both ends. Cut a 9" length of cording and tie knots at both ends. Tie around gardening tools. Use remaining cording to make a bow to go around flower mister similar to the one made above.

*Bumblebee Pattern*

*Ladybug Pattern*

*Butterfly Pattern*

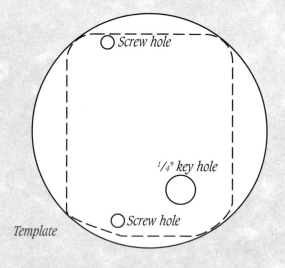

○ *Screw hole*

$1/4$" *key hole*

○ *Screw hole*

*Template*

# Thank Heaven

# *Brahms Lullaby*

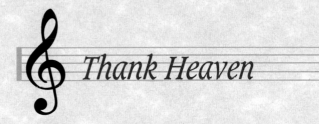

# Thank Heaven

## Materials Needed

*For the Base, Including Music Box Accessories:*
Dressed porcelain doll, 16" tall
Stuffed teddy bear, 8"
18-note key-wind
    miniature musical movement
Miniature T-bar winding key, $^7/_8$"

*Decorative Accessories for Music Box Pictured:*
Lapel pin, 2"
7mm pink silk ribbon, 12"
Quilting thread to match teddy bear color

*Tools:*
Needle
Seam ripper

## Step-by-Step Assembly

*Step One:*
    Using a seam ripper, carefully rip back center seam on teddy bear.

*Step Two:*
    Remove enough stuffing so the miniature musical movement will fit inside. Wind on miniature winding key. Place musical movement inside teddy bear.

*Step Three:*
    Using quilting thread, hand-sew seam halfway. Check to make sure musical movement fits snugly inside. It is important that the musical movement does not move around when it is wound. If necessary, add some of the stuffing back into teddy bear. Stitch seam closed.

*Photograph on page 41.*

*Step Four:*
    Tie silk ribbon around teddy bear's neck, making a bow in the back.

*Step Five:*
    Pin lapel pin to center front of teddy bear's neck on top of silk ribbon. Place teddy bear in the porcelain doll's arms.

# Brahms Lullaby

## Materials Needed

*For the Base, Including Music Box Accessories:*
Ceramic picture frame
Electronic miniature musical movement

*Adhesive:*
Industrial-strength glue

## Step-by-Step Assembly

*Step One:*
    Using industrial-strength glue, glue electronic musical movement to back of ceramic picture frame. Allow to dry thoroughly.

## Music Box Variations
    There are additional ideas for using electronic musical movements listed on page 58.

# *Wind Beneath My Wings*

# Materials Needed

## For the Base, Including Music Box Accessories:
Musical memento box,
    4$^1/_2$" wide x 3" deep x 2$^1/_2$" high
    with pre-drilled hole
18-note key-wind
    clear tone musical movement
T-bar winding key, $^1/_2$"
Sandpaper
Wood sealer

## Decorative Accessories for Music Box Pictured:
2 hand-blown glass birds, $^3/_4$"
Brass cone-shaped charm, 2$^1/_2$"
Brass decorative pull, $^7/_8$"
2 purple tassels, 1$^1/_2$"
1$^1/_4$"-wide flat ivory lace, 12"
1"-wide purple ombré wired ribbon, 25$^1/_2$"
4mm yellow silk ribbon, 7$^1/_2$"
Ivory thread
Purple thread
Yellow thread

## Acrylic Paint Color:
Lavender

## Adhesive and Spray Sealer:
Industrial-strength glue
Gloss spray sealer

## Tools and Brushes:
Hammer
Needle
Old paintbrush
Paintbrush
Scissors

*Pansy*

*Raw edge*

*Wired edge*

*Pansy Diagram*

# Step-by-Step Assembly

### Step One:
Using sandpaper, sand box. Refer to instructions for Sanding on page 14. Using an old paintbrush, apply wood sealer to box following manufacturer's directions. Allow to dry thoroughly.

### Step Two:
Using a paintbrush, paint box inside and out with lavender acrylic paint. Refer to instructions for Painting on page 14. Spray with two coats of gloss sealer, letting each coat dry before applying the next.

### Step Three:
Using ivory thread, hand-sew a gathering stitch along straight edge of ivory lace. Pull tightly to gather. Tie a few knots and trim threads.

### Step Four:
To make each pansy, cut an 8$^1/_2$" piece of wired ribbon. Cut in half lengthwise to make two 8$^1/_2$" x $^1/_2$" pieces. Cut one 3$^1/_2$"-wide piece and two 2$^1/_2$"-wide pieces from dark purple side of ribbon. Cut two 2$^1/_2$"-wide pieces from light purple side of ribbon. Using purple thread, tie a knot in end. Hand-sew a gathering stitch along cut edge of 3$^1/_2$" dark purple piece of ribbon. Refer to diagram at left. Do not sew too close to edge or ribbon will fray and tear. Do not cut thread. Gather two dark purple 2$^1/_2$" pieces the same way. Pull threads tightly. Stitch three petals together, forming a circle. Cut thread. Gather-stitch two 2$^1/_2$" light purple pieces the same way, but do not form a circle. Stitch light purple petals on top of two small dark purple petals. Shape flower. Cut a 2$^1/_2$" piece of yellow silk ribbon, and sew, using yellow thread, a gathering stitch very close to one long edge of ribbon. Pull threads tight and secure. Tack to center of pansy. Sew two more pansies the same way.

### Step Five:
Carefully hammer decorative pull on center front of lid. Tie tassels onto brass ring on decorative pull.

### Step Six:
Using industrial-strength glue, glue clear tone musical movement in bottom of box, making sure winding-key shaft is centered in hole. Glue cone-shaped charm to top of lid, lace on top edge of cone, and pansies on lace, referring to photograph for placement. Glue glass birds to side of cone. Allow to dry thoroughly. Wind on winding key.

# *Those Were the Days*

## Materials Needed

### For the Base, Including Music Box Accessories:
Oval chipboard box, 2$\frac{1}{2}$" high x 17$\frac{1}{2}$" circumference
Oval chipboard box, 2$\frac{1}{4}$" high x 14" circumference
Oval chipboard box, 2" high x 11" circumference
18-note key-wind musical movement
Triangle ring winding key, $\frac{3}{4}$"

### Decorative Accessories for Music Box Pictured:
Gold-tone double-cherub charm
2 gold-tone roses with leaves charms
Ceramic bonnet, 3$\frac{1}{2}$" wide x 4" long x 1" high
Wooden knob, $\frac{1}{2}$"
Burgundy velvet, $\frac{1}{4}$ yard
15 green velvet leaves
2"-wide dusty-rose craft ribbon, 18"
2"-wide floral craft ribbon, 14$\frac{1}{2}$"
1$\frac{1}{2}$"-wide burgundy craft ribbon, 11$\frac{1}{2}$"
$\frac{1}{2}$"-wide off-white trim, 1$\frac{1}{2}$ yards
$\frac{5}{8}$"-wide burgundy wire ribbon, 27"
2"-wide off-white pointed lace, 20"
4mm light green silk ribbon, 1 yard
4mm light pink silk ribbon, 1 yard
4mm mauve silk ribbon, 1 yard
4mm medium green silk ribbon, 1 yard
4mm rose silk ribbon, 1 yard
Invisible thread

### Acrylic Paint Colors:
Brown
Burgundy
Dark green
Light green
Metallic gold
Off-white
Rose

### Adhesives and Spray Sealer:
Hot glue sticks
Industrial-strength glue
Tacky glue
Tacky glue, thin-bodied
Gloss spray sealer

### Tools and Brushes:
Drill with $\frac{1}{4}$" drill bit
Glue gun
Needle
Old clean rag
Old paintbrush
Paintbrushes
Paper towels
Scissors

## Step-by-Step Assembly

### Step One:
Prepare chipboard boxes. Refer to instructions for Preparing Boxes on page 14. Using thin-bodied Tacky glue, laminate dusty-rose ribbon to side of large box, floral ribbon to side of medium box, and burgundy ribbon to side of small box. Refer to instructions for Laminating on page 13.

### Step Two:
Using a paintbrush, paint box lids, knob, and ceramic bonnet with rose acrylic paint. Refer to instructions for Painting on page 14. Spray with gloss sealer.

### Step Three:
One at a time, paint charms with off-white. Before paint dries, wipe paint off with an old clean rag leaving paint in crevices. Allow to dry thoroughly. Spray with gloss sealer.

### Step Four:
Dry-brush bonnet with off-white. Refer to instructions for Dry Brushing on page 13. Paint ribbon on bonnet with burgundy. Allow to dry thoroughly. Spray with gloss sealer.

### Step Five:
To make burgundy velvet rosebuds, cut out 17 velvet circles 3$\frac{1}{2}$" in diameter. Fold circles in half with wrong sides together. With folded edge up, fold into thirds, overlapping sides with raw edges aligned. Using invisible thread, hand-sew a gathering stitch. Refer to diagram on page 48. Gather tightly. Wrap thread around stitch to secure.

**Step Six:**

Drill a $1/4$" hole at back of large box $3/4$" from box bottom and $3/4$" from back center. Using industrial-strength glue, glue musical movement to inside of box, making sure winding-key shaft is centered in hole. Allow to dry thoroughly.

**Step Seven:**

Dry-brush velvet rosebuds with burgundy and along folded edge with metallic gold. Dry-brush velvet leaves with dark green, then light green over dark green, and the edges of the leaves with brown.

**Step Eight:**

Using Tacky glue, glue lids on boxes. Using a glue gun, hot-glue medium box on top center of large box. Glue small box on top center of medium box. Be sure all ribbon and lid seams are in the back.

**Step Nine:**

Centering, hot-glue off-white trim on sides of all three lids. Be sure seams are at the center back. Tie wire ribbon around boxes, top to bottom. Refer to photograph. Making sure ribbon is tight, glue to top of small box.

**Step Ten:**

Turn boxes upside down. Hot-glue pointed lace around bottom edge of large box, making sure it lies flat and seam is in the back. Turn boxes back over.

**Step Eleven:**

Overlapping, hot-glue velvet leaves around edge of small box. Refer to photograph. Place bonnet on top of knob and position on small box. Remove bonnet and, using industrial-strength glue, glue knob in place. Hot-glue eight rosebuds around the top edge of box. Glue five rosebuds on top of eight. Glue three rosebuds on top of five. Glue last rosebud on top of three. Refer to photograph.

**Step Twelve:**

Handling the five lengths of silk ribbon as one, tie a small bow at center. Hot-glue to front of boxes. Cascade ribbons down front of boxes, tieing knots in ribbon every 3" to $3^1/2$". Tack knots in place with hot glue. Tie a knot in ribbon tails 1" from the last place ribbon was tacked down with glue. Refer to photograph. Trim ribbons 1" from knots.

**Step Thirteen:**

Using industrial-strength glue, glue on charms. Glue bonnet on top of knob. Refer to photograph. Allow to dry thoroughly. Wind on winding key.

## Music Box Variations

- To create this music box quicker and simpler than the one pictured on page 46, use printed hat boxes instead of laminating chipboard boxes. On the top of the hat boxes, make a small dried or silk floral arrangement.

- Turn this music box into one to remind you of fond vacation at the beach memories. Use printed hat boxes or, if preferred, laminate chipboard boxes. Refer to instructions for Laminating on page 13. Using industrial strength glue, glue a variety of seashells onto the top of the stack of hat boxes.

- Turn this music box into one featuring sewing or knitting. Use printed hat boxes or, if preferred, laminate chipboard boxes. Refer to instructions for Laminating on page 13. Using industrial-strength glue, glue wooden spools, decorative scissors, fancy hat pins, needles, balls of yarn, and knitting needles onto the top of the stack of hat boxes. Refer to "Love Story" on page 27 for a list of similar materials, as well as instructions for making fancy hat pins on page 32.

*Rosebud Diagram*

48

# Tea for Two

## Materials Needed

### For the Base, Including Music Box Accessories:
Round floral-print hat box, 2$\frac{1}{2}$" high x 5$\frac{1}{2}$" diameter
18-note key-wind musical movement
Top-mount rotation assembly
Left-hand threaded turntable, 1"
Left-hand threaded-shaft extender, $\frac{3}{8}$"
Left-hand threaded-shaft extender, $\frac{1}{2}$"
T-bar winding key, $\frac{3}{4}$"
4 wooden finials, 2"

### Decorative Accessories for Music Box Pictured:
Miniature tea set
2 miniature spoons
Miniature knife
White Battenburg doily, 8" square
Small amount of tan sculpting clay
2 crocheted hats, 1"
2 squares of blue cotton fabric, 1$\frac{1}{4}$" x 1$\frac{1}{4}$"
2 silver square beads, $\frac{1}{4}$"
4mm blue silk ribbon, 12"
4mm pink silk ribbon, 12"
Tea dye or tea bags

### Acrylic Paint Colors, Acrylic Enamel Paint, and Glass Paint:
Pink to match hat box
Blue to match hat box
White gloss acrylic enamel
Tea-colored glass paint

### Adhesives and Spray Sealer:
Hot glue sticks
Industrial-strength glue
Tacky glue
Gloss spray sealer

### Tools and Brushes:
Drill with $\frac{1}{4}$" and $\frac{1}{2}$" drill bits
Glue gun
Old paintbrushes
Paintbrush
Paper towels
Scissors
Strong rubber band

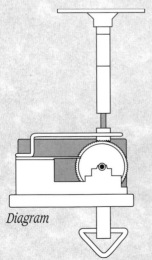

*Diagram*

## Step-by-Step Assembly

### Step One:
Tea-dye doily. Refer to instructions of Tea Dyeing on page 16.

### Step Two:
Drill a $\frac{1}{2}$" hole 1$\frac{1}{4}$" from edge of lid. Attach top-mount rotation assembly to musical movement following manufacturer's directions. Referring to diagram at left, wind left-hand threaded-shaft extenders onto top-mount rotation assembly. To mark winding-key hole, place musical movement inside box. It is very important that the left-hand threaded-shaft extender is centered in the hole in the lid. Remove lid. Draw a line around musical movement. Remove musical movement, and paint a small dot of paint on the bottom of the winding-key shaft. Press musical movement back into box so dot of paint marks placement for hole, and remove once hole has been marked. Drill a $\frac{1}{4}$" hole, using paint dot as the center mark. Using industrial-strength glue, glue musical movement into box, making sure winding-key shaft is centered in hole. Using Tacky glue, glue lid on box, lining up hole in lid over left-hand threaded-shaft extenders. Allow to dry thoroughly.

### Step Three:
Using tan sculpting clay, roll seven small balls to make snacks — make sure they are the appropriate size for the plate. Flatten slightly. Bake clay following manufacturer's directions. Allow to cool thoroughly. Spray with gloss sealer.

### Step Four:
Using a glue gun, fill teacups and creamer with hot glue to just below rim. Allow to harden and cool thoroughly.

### Step Five:
Dry-brush one crocheted hat with pink acrylic paint and one crocheted hat with blue. Refer to instructions for Dry Brushing on page 13.

**Step Six:**

Fray edges of both 1¼" fabric squares. Starting at one corner, roll up and slide into square beads to make napkins and napkin rings. Put a small dot of Tacky glue on each "napkin" under bead. Allow to dry thoroughly.

**Step Seven:**

Using an old paintbrush, apply a thin layer of Tacky glue to top and side of lid. Refer to photograph. Press doily on top and sides. Making sure point on doily is in the proper place from turntable hole, cut a ¼" hole in doily over hole in top of lid. Press fabric inside the hole. Using a strong rubber band, place it around the sides of box to hold doily in place. Allow to dry thoroughly. When dry, remove rubber band.

**Step Eight:**

Using a paintbrush, paint finials with pink and blue acrylic paints. Refer to instructions for Painting on page 14. Refer to the photograph. Spray with gloss sealer.

**Step Nine:**

Using an old paintbrush, paint the hot glue in creamer with white gloss acrylic enamel and the hot glue in teacups with tea-colored glass paint. Allow to dry thoroughly.

**Step Ten:**

Using industrial-strength glue, glue finials, evenly spaced, to bottom of box for legs. Refer to photograph. Allow to dry thoroughly.

**Step Eleven:**

Wind left-hand threaded turntable onto left-hand threaded-shaft extenders. Glue teapot on turntable and glue the lids on teapot and sugar bowl and the "clay" snacks and knife on one plate. Glue snack plate, cups, saucers, sugar bowl, creamer, napkins, spoons, and hats on table top, referring to diagram at right for placement.

**Step Twelve:**

Tie a small bow in the center of each silk ribbon. Tie a knot at the center of each tail. Glue bows to hats and knots to the edge of lid. Wind on winding key.

## Music Box Variations

- Instead of making the setting on this table similar to that of a "tea party," try substituting the decorative accessories with ones more appropriate for that of a teenager's table. Start with a red and white checked tablecloth. What would be more appropriate than pizza and cola or maybe an ice cream soda to share.

- Instead of making the setting on this table similar to that of a "tea party," try substituting the decorative accessories with ones similar to a "Thanksgiving" dinner, such as turkey, cranberries, and dinner rolls. Don't forget the pumpkin pie.

- Instead of making the setting on this table similar to that of a "tea party," try substituting the decorative accessories with ones similar to a "Christmas" dinner. Pull out the good china and stemware, and don't forget to have candlelight and a beautiful centerpiece complete with poinsettias and holly.

*Diagram*

## Materials Needed

### For the Base, Including Music Box Accessories:
Oval wicker basket, 11" high (including handle) x 32" circumference
Hardboard, 14" x 8" x $\frac{1}{8}$" thick
18-note key-wind miniature musical movement
Miniature turntable, 3"

### Decorative Accessories for Music Box Pictured:
2 prepainted resin sitting teddy bear figurines, 1$\frac{1}{2}$" high
Small wicker basket, 1$\frac{1}{4}$"
Miniature pie
Assortment of miniature fruits
Wooden candle cup, $\frac{1}{2}$"
Floral-print fabric, $\frac{1}{3}$ yard
Red-and-white small check fabric, 5" circle
Lightweight cardboard
Thick batting, $\frac{1}{4}$ yard
1$\frac{1}{4}$"-wide flat crocheted lace, 1$\frac{1}{2}$ yards
$\frac{5}{8}$"-wide dark green grosgrain ribbon, 2 yards
$\frac{1}{2}$"-wide off-white fringe, 11"
Off-white quilting thread
Small silk sunflowers
Small off-white silk flowers
Silk greenery vine with miniature leaves, 1 yard

### Glass Paint and Stain:
Yellow glass paint
Medium walnut stain

### Adhesives:
Hot glue sticks
Industrial-strength glue
Tacky glue

### Tools and Brushes:
Glue gun
Needle
Old paintbrushes
Saw
Scissors
Twist ties

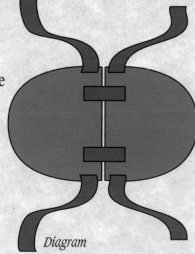

*Diagram*

## Step-by-Step Assembly

### Step One:
Draw a pattern for both sides of basket lid, referring to photograph. It is likely that each side will be different. Transfer patterns to hardboard. Refer to instructions for Transferring on page 16. Using a saw, cut out each side.

### Step Two:
Using industrial-strength glue, glue musical movement to one side of hardboard lid, centering, making sure winding-key shaft is pointing up.

### Step Three:
Using the hardboard pieces as a pattern, cut two layers of thick batting for each side. Cut two pieces from lightweight cardboard.

### Step Four:
Place batting on the side of lid that has musical movement. Trim around musical movement. Apply a thin layer of Tacky glue to lid sides, and place batting on top. Allow to dry thoroughly.

### Step Five:
Using the hardboard pieces as a pattern, cut two pieces from floral-print fabric 1$\frac{1}{2}$" larger on all sides. Place fabric pieces, right sides down. Centering, place hardboard pieces, batting side down, on top of fabric. Snugly wrap sides over hardboard and, using a glue gun, hot-glue in place. Using the cardboard pieces as a pattern, cut two pieces from floral-print fabric $\frac{1}{2}$" larger on all sides. Place fabric pieces, right sides down. Centering, place cardboard pieces on top of fabric. Snugly wrap sides over cardboard and hot-glue in place.

### Step Six:
Cut crocheted lace into two $\frac{3}{4}$-yard lengths. Using quilting thread, hand-sew a gathering stitch along straight edges of lace. Gather to fit around curved edges of lids. Hot-glue to bottom sides on curved edges of lids — not on straight edges. Place lids, fabric sides down, and straight edges together. Cut two 2" pieces from grosgrain ribbon. Glue grosgrain ribbon to lid sides to make hinges. Refer to diagram.

### Step Seven:

Cut remaining grosgrain ribbon into four equal lengths. Hot-glue 1" to lids for ties. Glue cardboard lining pieces, right side up, over ribbons and lace. Place lids on basket and tie ribbons around handles. Tie a bow around each handle.

### Step Eight:

Turning edges under $1/4$" on red-and-white check fabric, hand-sew a gathering stitch $1/8$" from edge using quilting thread. Place right side down. Center miniature turntable on fabric with winding-key shaft pointing up. Gather tightly and tie a few knots. Trim ends. Glue fringe around bottom edge.

### Step Nine:

To make the "honey pot," stain candle cup. Refer to instructions for Staining on pages 15-16. When stain is thoroughly dry, using a glue gun, fill candle cup with hot glue, allowing glue to drip over top rim. Allow to harden and cool thoroughly. Refer to photograph. Using an old paintbrush, paint the hot glue in candle cup with yellow glass paint. Allow to dry thoroughly.

### Step Ten:

Trim fabric around winding-key shaft on lid. Wind miniature turntable onto winding-key shaft. Using industrial-strength glue, glue teddy bear figurines, small wicker basket, and honey pot on top of the turntable. Glue pie and a few pieces of fruit to fabric and the remaining fruit in the small wicker basket. The turntable is the winding key. Allow to dry thoroughly. Refer to photograph.

### Step Eleven:

Using industrial-strength glue, glue greenery vine to basket handle and around to front of basket. Use a few twist ties to secure vine in place until glue has dried thoroughly. Allow to dry thoroughly. Refer to photograph. When dry, remove twist ties.

### Step Twelve:

Using a glue gun, hot-glue silk sunflowers and small off-white silk flowers to top of basket. Glue ribbon tails to basket, twisting every few inches. Refer to photograph.

# Wedding March

## Materials Needed

*For the Base, Including Music Box Accessories:*
Round chipboard box, $2^{1}/4$" high x 5" diameter
Round chipboard box, $1^{1}/2$" high x $3^{1}/2$" diameter
Cake plate, 8"
18-note key-wind musical movement
Turntable, 3"

*Decorative Accessories for Music Box Pictured:*
Prepainted bride and groom figurine(s), 2" tall
Plastic standing heart cake decoration, 3"
White jacquard fabric, $1/4$ yard
$3/4$"-wide scalloped flat pleated lace, 30"
1"-wide pleated satin ruffle, 18"
Pleated icing satin ribbon, $1^{1}/3$ yard
$1/2$"- wide scalloped wedding lace, 12"
$1^{1}/2$"-wide scalloped wedding lace, 18"
5 silk flower sprays, 6"

*Acrylic Paint Color:*
White

*Adhesives and Spray Sealer:*
Hot glue sticks
Industrial-strength glue
Tacky glue
Tacky glue, thin-bodied
Matte spray sealer

*Tools and Brushes:*
Drill with $1/4$" drill bit
Glue gun
Old paintbrush
Paintbrush
Scissors

*Continued on page 56.*

# *Wedding March*

Continued from page 54.

## Step-by-Step Assembly

### Step One:

Prepare chipboard boxes. Refer to instructions for Preparing Boxes on page 14.

### Step Two:

Cut two strips: one 2" x 16" and another 1³/₄" x 11¹/₄", and two circles: one 5" and another 3¹/₂", from white jacquard fabric. Using thin-bodied Tacky glue, laminate fabric strips to sides of boxes. Make sure bottom edges are even. Wrap ¹/₄" of excess fabric on small box to inside and glue down. Laminate fabric circles to box bottoms. Refer to instructions for Laminating on page 13.

### Step Three:

Drill a ¹/₄" hole in center of lid on large box. The small box lid will not be used.

### Step Four:

Using a paintbrush, paint the outside of lid with white acrylic paint. Refer to instructions for Painting on page 14. Spray with matte sealer.

### Step Five:

Using industrial-strength glue, glue turntable to center of cake plate with the shaft sticking up. Glue musical movement to inside of lid, centering winding-key shaft in hole. Using Tacky glue, glue lid on box. Allow to dry thoroughly.

### Step Six:

Turn boxes over. Bottom of boxes will now be referred to as top of boxes. Using a glue gun, hot-glue scalloped flat pleated lace around the bottom, open end, of small box. Glue remaining lace around the bottom edge (lid) of large box. Glue pleated satin ruffle on top of scalloped flat pleated lace on large box only so it is on the bottom. Glue pleated icing satin ribbon around the top edge of small and large boxes and around the side of lid at bottom of large box. Glue ¹/₂" scalloped wedding lace around sides of small box and 1¹/₂" scalloped wedding lace around sides of

large box. Glue bottom open end of small box to the top center of large box. Refer to photograph.

### Step Seven:

Using industrial-strength glue, glue plastic standing heart cake decoration and bride and groom figurine(s) to top of cake. Allow to dry thoroughly.

### Step Eight:

Glue two flower sprays to the front of plastic heart and two to the back by placing large end of flower spray at bottom of heart and curving it toward center of heart. Cascade remaining flower spray down left side of bride and groom, referring to photograph.

### Step Nine:

Wind cake onto turntable. The turntable is the winding key.

### Note:

To wash cake plate, remove cake from turntable.

## Music Box Variations

- Instead of making this music box into a wedding cake, try a birthday cake. Two layers are not necessary, but can be used. To replicate frosting roses, small porcelain or ceramic roses can be used. To make candles, simply cut thin dowels into an appropriate length. Sand if necessary, and paint with acrylic paint. Refer to instructions for Sanding on page 14 and for Painting on page 14. For the "wick," glue a small piece of white string to the center top of painted dowels. Cut the stem from a "Happy Birthday" floral pick and glue it to the top of the birthday cake. If the cake is for a child, it can be decorated with prepainted plastic or resin clowns and balloons. Use a bright-colored ribbon as the icing to go around the edges. Of course, an "Over-the-Hill" cake can be made by simply using black jacquard fabric instead of white. Using white puff paint, carefully print sentiments to the birthday honoree.

# Hawaiian Wedding Song

## Materials Needed

*For the Base, Including Music Box Accessories:*
Teddy
Electronic miniature musical movement

*Decorative Accessories for Music Box Pictured:*
Coordinating fabric, 3" x 7"
Matching thread

*Tools:*
Iron
Sewing machine

## Step-by-Step Assembly

*Step One:*
Make a pouch for musical movement by turning and pressing both 3" edges of fabric under ¹/₄". Turn over another ¹/₄" and press again. Using a sewing machine, sew a ¹/₄" seam on both edges, with matching thread.

*Step Two:*
Fold fabric, right sides together, referring to diagram below. Sew a ¹/₄" seam along both unfinished edges. Finish off raw edges and turn right side out.

*Step Three:*
Using a medium zig-zag stitch, and stretching waistband, sew one folded edge on pouch to the inside of waist on teddy, halfway between center and side seams. Insert electronic musical movement so the button is facing outward.

*Note:*
Remove musical movement before laundering.

*Pouch Diagram*

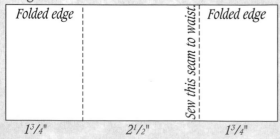

## Music Box Variations

Alter this music box for any number of gift-giving occasions.

• Using the assembly instructions for making a pouch, sew one into the waistband of a festive pair of boxer shorts. Place an electronic musical movement into the pouch. What a great gift idea for Father's Day or Christmas!

• Using the assembly instructions for making a pouch, sew one into the waistband of a Halloween costume. Place an electronic musical movement into the pouch. There are many Halloween tunes to choose from.

• Using the assembly instructions for making a pouch, sew one into a child's pillowcase. What a great way to get those kids into bed on time!

• Using the assembly instructions for making a pouch, sew one into a child's winter coat. This provides company for the child on those long walks home from school. Change the tunes for the different holidays.

• Using industrial-strength glue, glue an electronic musical movement at the back of a photo frame for a wedding or baby-shower gift.

• Using industrial-strength glue, glue an electronic musical movement in a jewelry box lid for any special occasion for Mom.

• Using industrial-strength glue, glue an electronic musical movement in a lunch box — what a fun experience at lunchtime!

• Using Tacky glue, glue an electronic musical movement on top of a present. When handing the recipient the gift, press the musical movement and enjoy the reaction!

# *Ebb Tide*

## Materials Needed

### For the Base, Including Music Box Accessories:
Wicker fishing basket,
    $8^1/_2$" wide x $5^1/_2$" deep x 4" high
18-note key-wind musical movement
T-bar winding key, $^3/_4$"

### Decorative Accessories for Music Box Pictured:
Prepainted resin fishing bear, 2"
5 ceramic trees, (2) 3", (3) 2"
Wooden sign with jagged-cut edges,
    3" x $1^1/_4$" x $^1/_4$"
2 prepainted wooden fish, $1^1/_4$"
Cotton rope, 8"
2 two-ounce packages of
    light blue pearl sculpting clay

### Acrylic Paint Colors and Antiquing Gel:
Dark green
Medium green
Off-white
White
Brown antiquing gel

### Adhesives and Spray Sealers:
Industrial-strength glue
Wood glue
Gloss spray sealer
Matte spray sealer

### Tools and Brushes:
Aluminum foil or plastic wrap
Ceramic cleaning tool
Fine-point permanent black marker
Old clean rag
Old paintbrush
Paintbrush
Paper towels
X-acto knife

GONE
*Lettering*   FISHIN

## Step-by-Step Assembly

### Step One:
Using an X-acto knife, cut a small hole in the back center bottom of fishing basket to accommodate winding-key shaft.

### Step Two:
Using industrial-strength glue, glue musical movement inside basket. Center winding-key shaft and wind on winding key. Allow to dry thoroughly. A small amount of wood glue might be needed on cut wicker around winding-key shaft.

### Step Three:
Using an old paintbrush, antique ceramic tree trunks with brown antiquing gel. Refer to instructions for Antiquing on page 12.

### Step Four:
Sculpt river from sculpting clay. Refer to instructions for Sculpting Clay Water on pages 14-15.

### Step Five:
Using a paintbrush, paint treetops with dark green acrylic paint. Paint sign with off-white and edges with dark green. Refer to instructions for Painting on page 14. Transfer lettering at left onto sign. Refer to instructions for Transferring on page 16. Using a permanent marker, write "Gone Fishin" on sign.

### Step Six:
Dry-brush water peaks with white. Dry-brush treetops with medium green. Refer to instructions for Dry Brushing on page 13. Spray sculpted river and trees with gloss sealer. Spray "Gone Fishin" sign with matte sealer.

### Step Seven:
Using industrial-strength glue, glue fish and rope to sign. Refer to photograph. Glue sign and sculpted river to basket. Position all trees and fishing bear on basket, and, one at a time, glue on. Allow to dry thoroughly.

# Old MacDonald

## Materials Needed

### For the Base, Including Music Box Accessories:
Round heavy-duty wooden basket,
  7" high (including handle)
  x 6" diameter with a 1/2" top rim
Plywood, 6" x 6" x 1/4" thick
18-note key-wind musical movement
Top-mount rotation assembly
Left-hand threaded turntable, 3"
Left-hand threaded-shaft extender, 1"
T-bar winding key, 3/8"
Textured snow
Sandpaper
Wood sealer

### Decorative Accessories for Music Box Pictured:
Prepainted figurines (resin or ceramic),
  7/8" to 1 1/2" high:
    Cow
    Duck
    Pig
    Rooster
    Sheep
    Water pump
Block of wood,
  2" wide x 3" high x 2 1/4" thick
Wagon wheel, 2"
Wooden picket fence wired together,
  1" high x 19" long

### Acrylic Paint Colors:
  Black
  Brown
  Dark green
  Gray
  Light green
  Off-white
  Red

### Adhesive and Spray Sealer:
  Industrial-strength glue
  Gloss spray sealer

*Diagram*

### Tools and Brushes:
  Drill with 1/4" drill bit
  Old paintbrushes
  Paintbrush
  Paper towels
  Ruler
  Saw

## Step-by-Step Assembly

### Step One:
Using a ruler, measure the diameter of the inside of the basket across the top to get an exact measurement. Using that measurement less 1/4", draw a circle on plywood. Transfer barn patterns on page 63 to block of wood. Refer to instructions for Transferring on page 16. Using a saw, cut circle and barn out.

### Step Two:
Using an old paintbrush, apply textured snow to top and sides of plywood circle following manufacturer's directions. Allow to dry thoroughly.

### Step Three:
If necessary, use sandpaper to sand basket and barn. Refer to instructions for Sanding on page 14. Using an old paintbrush, apply wood sealer to basket and barn following manufacturer's directions. Allow to dry thoroughly.

### Step Four:
Using a paintbrush, paint textured snow and sides of basket with dark green acrylic paint. Paint handle, top rim, and bottom rim of basket with brown. Paint barn with red and roof with black. Allow to dry thoroughly. Transfer barn door and window patterns on page 63. Paint details on barn, referring to patterns for paint colors. Paint spokes on wagon wheel with red, center of and outer wheel with black. Paint picket fence with off-white. Refer to instructions for Painting on page 14.

**Step Five:**

Dry-brush textured snow with light green. Refer to instructions for Dry Brushing on page 13. Spray basket, barn, fence, wagon wheel, and textured snow with gloss sealer.

**Step Six:**

Attach top-mount rotation assembly to musical movement following manufacturer's directions. Referring to diagram on page 62, wind left-hand threaded-shaft extender onto top-mount rotation assembly. To mark winding-key hole, place musical movement inside basket. It is very important that the left-hand threaded-shaft extender is centered in basket. Draw a line around musical movement. Remove musical movement, and paint a small dot of paint on the bottom of the winding-key shaft. Press musical movement back into basket so dot of paint marks placement for hole, and remove once hole has been marked. Drill a $1/4$" hole using paint dot as the center mark. Using industrial-strength glue, glue musical movement into basket, making sure winding-key shaft is centered in hole. Glue left-hand threaded turntable to center bottom of plywood circle. Allow to dry thoroughly. Wind turntable onto left-hand threaded-shaft extender.

**Step Seven:**

Using industrial-strength glue, glue picket fence around basket. Glue wagon wheel on fence. Refer to photograph for placement. Glue back of barn on back center rim of basket, but do not glue front of barn to "grass." Allow to dry thoroughly.

**Step Eight:**

Wind winding key onto winding-key shaft so music is playing. Place animals and water pump on top of grass. Refer to photograph for placement. Move animals as needed so they move smoothly through barn without bumping into it. When they are positioned correctly, glue in place. Allow to dry thoroughly.

## Music Box Variation

- Instead of making this music box into a barnyard scene, make it into one that every train collector would love. The pattern provided for the barn will work to create a mountain. Using instant papier-mâché, apply to wood until it looks like a mountain. Arrange the top of the box so that a train can go around and through the "tunnel." Cut the pointed ends off the wooden picket fence and paint with black acrylic paint for a train track. Miscellaneous railroad crossing signs can be glued to the top of the box using industrial strength glue.

Barn Pattern

Barn — Side View Pattern

Back of Barn

# Materials Needed

## For the Base, Including Music Box Accessories:
Oval shaker box, 3" high x 22" circumference
18-note key-wind musical movement
T-bar winding key, $^3/_4$"
Sandpaper
Wood sealer

## Decorative Accessories for Music Box Pictured:
4 French-style wooden plaques,
   (2) 6" x 7$^1/_2$", (1) 4" x 6", (1) 3" x 4"
Wooden block, 1$^1/_2$" x 1$^1/_2$" x 3"
Wooden ring, 1"
Copper, 2" x 2$^1/_2$"
Wooden boy peg, 1$^1/_4$"
6 sets hand-carved wooden animals,
   approximately 1" to 1$^1/_4$" high
2 small birds
Small amount of Spanish moss
Textured snow
4 two-ounce packages of
   light blue pearl sculpting clay

## Acrylic Paint Colors and Stain:
Black
Blue-gray
Caucasian flesh-tone
Country-blue
Dark blue
Dark green
Dark red
Pink
White
Light walnut stain

## Adhesives and Spray Sealers:
Industrial-strength glue
Tacky glue
Wood glue
Gloss spray sealer
Matte spray sealer

## Tools and Brushes:
Aluminum foil or plastic wrap
Ceramic cleaning tool
Clamps
Drill with $^1/_4$" drill bit
Fine-point permanent black marker
Old paintbrushes
Paintbrushes
Paper towels
Saw

# Step-by-Step Assembly

### Step One:
Using sandpaper, sand box and plaques. Refer to instructions for Sanding on page 14. Using an old paintbrush, apply wood sealer to box following manufacturer's directions. Allow to dry thoroughly.

### Step Two:
Using a paintbrush, paint box with dark blue acrylic paint. Refer to instructions for Painting on page 14. Spray with matte sealer.

### Step Three:
Mark center cutout on one of the largest plaques. Refer to diagram on page 66. Mark roof line on wooden block. Refer to diagram on page 66. Using a saw, cut along lines.

### Step Four:
Using an old paintbrush, stain three plaques and wooden ring with stain. Do not stain plaque with cutout. Using a paintbrush, stain plaque with cutout with dark red acrylic paint and block with dark green. Refer to instructions for Staining on pages 15-16. Allow to dry thoroughly.

### Step Five:
Sculpt water from sculpting clay. Refer to instructions for Sculpting Clay Water on pages 14-15. Place small plaque on top center of box, making sure clay extends to outer edge of box. Mark around plaque — the inside area should not be sculpted.

### Step Six:

Dry-brush water peaks with white. Refer to instructions for Dry Brushing on page 13. Spray with gloss sealer.

### Step Seven:

Place ring on front of block. Refer to photograph. Draw a line around center of ring and remove it. Paint circle with blue-gray.

### Step Eight:

Using wood glue, glue plaques together — small, medium, large, and, finally, large with cutout. Refer to photograph. Clamp and allow to dry thoroughly. Glue ring onto block over painted circle. Glue block to top center of "ark." Allow to dry thoroughly.

### Step Nine:

Stain boy peg — head with flesh-tone and body with country-blue acrylic paints, referring to photograph. Draw arms and hands on peg. Refer to "Noah" pattern below. Paint hands with flesh-tone. Using a permanent marker, outline arms and hands. Using the end of a small paintbrush, dot on eyes with black. Paint mouth and dot nose with pink. Wash cheeks with pink. Place a small highlight dot in each eye with white.

### Step Ten:

Using an old paintbrush (small), apply textured snow for hair, beard, mustache, and eyebrows on "Noah" following manufacturer's directions. Allow to dry thoroughly. Spray "Noah" and his "ark" with matte sealer.

### Step Eleven:

Drill a 1/4" hole in back center of box, centering winding-key shaft. Using industrial-strength glue, glue musical movement in place. Allow to dry thoroughly.

### Step Twelve:

Using Tacky glue, glue lid on box. Using industrial-strength glue, glue sculpted water to top of box. Glue "ark" on top of water. Bend copper in half to fit roof and glue it on. Allow to dry thoroughly.

### Step Thirteen:

Using Spanish moss, form a small bird's nest. Using industrial-strength glue, glue nest to top of roof and glue birds inside nest. Glue hand-carved animals on "ark," referring to photograph for placement. Glue "Noah" in cutout opening. Allow to dry thoroughly. Wind on winding key.

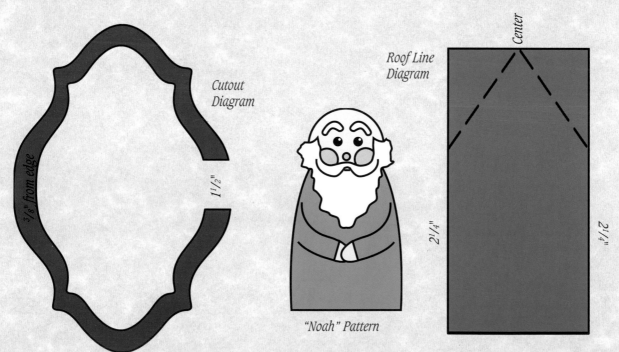

Cutout Diagram

3/8" from edge

1 1/2"

"Noah" Pattern

Roof Line Diagram

Center

2 1/4"

2 1/4"

# Country Roads

## Materials Needed

### For the Base, Including Music Box Accessories:
Round papier-mâché box, 3" high x 7" diameter
Round wooden plaque, 7" diameter x $3/4$" thick
Square of wood, 2" x 2" x $1/2$" thick
18-note key-wind musical movement
Left-hand threaded-shaft
Left-hand threaded turntable, 3"
2 key extenders, $1^1/_2$"
Triangle ring winding key, $3/4$"
Découpage
Sandpaper

### Decorative Accessories for Music Box Pictured:
4 miniature bales of hay
Miniature saddle
6 horseshoes, 1"
Finishing nail, $1^1/_2$"
Red cowboy hat, 2"
Red cowboy boots, $1^1/_2$"
Prepainted cow skull, 1"
Pitchfork
2 prepainted dogs
Wooden barrel, $1^1/_2$"
Wagon wheel, $1^3/_4$"
15 silver conchos, $3/4$"
Silver concho, $1^1/_2$"
Tan sculpting clay
$1/4$"-wide brown ultra-suede or leather, 22"
Light blue denim, $3^1/_2$" x 22" strip
Light blue denim, $8^1/_2$" circle
Heavyweight cardboard, $7^1/_2$" circle
Rope, 1 yard
Cotton rope, 18"

### Acrylic Paint Colors, Acrylic Enamel Paint, Antiquing Gel, and Stain:
Black
Red
Black gloss acrylic enamel
Black antiquing gel
Medium walnut stain

### Adhesives and Spray Sealers:
Industrial-strength glue
Tacky glue
Tacky glue, thin-bodied
Gloss spray sealer
Matte spray sealer

### Tools and Brushes:
Drill with $1/4$" and $1/2$" drill bits
Hammer
Old clean rag
Old paintbrushes
Paintbrushes
Straight pin

## Step-by-Step Assembly

### Step One:
Using thin-bodied Tacky glue, laminate denim strip to side of box, centering it, and denim circle to cardboard circle. Refer to instructions for Laminating on page 13.

### Step Two:
Using an old paintbrush, brush a coat of découpage over bales of hay, being careful not to break off too much hay. Allow to dry thoroughly.

### Step Three:
Using a paintbrush, paint box lid with red acrylic paint. Refer to instructions for Painting on page 14. Spray with gloss sealer.

### Step Four:
Using sandpaper, sand plaque. Refer to instructions for Sanding on page 14. Using an old paintbrush, stain plaque and barrel. Refer to instructions for Staining on pages 15-16. Using a paintbrush, paint rings around barrel with black acrylic paint. Spray with matte sealer.

### Step Five:
Drill a $1/2$" hole in center lid top for turntable. Drill a $1/4$" hole at box back $1/4$" from back seam and $1^1/_8$" from box bottom to accommodate winding key. Push left-hand threaded-shaft into the accessory hole

on side of musical movement. Wind key extenders together, and wind onto winding-key shaft. Using industrial-strength glue, glue 2" square of wood into bottom center of box and musical movement on top of 2" square of wood, making sure winding-key shaft is centered in hole. Wind winding key onto key extenders through side hole at back of box. Refer to diagram on page 70. Place lid on box, making sure left-hand threaded-shaft is in the center of turntable hole. Place denim cardboard circle base, denim side down, and centering, glue box bottom to top of cardboard circle. Glue left-hand threaded turntable to center of plaque bottom. Allow to dry thoroughly.

### Step Six:

Using an old paintbrush, antique all conchos with black antiquing gel. Refer to instructions for Antiquing on page 12. Spray with gloss sealer.

### Step Seven:

Using Tacky glue, glue lid on box. Centering, glue ultra-suede around lid side. Allow to dry thoroughly.

### Step Eight:

Using industrial-strength glue, glue $^3/_4$" conchos, evenly spaced, around side of lid. Glue rope around base. Tie knots in ends of rope. Glue $1^1/_2$" concho on top of rope. Refer to photograph. Allow to dry thoroughly.

### Step Nine:

Using tan sculpting clay, sculpt a small snake. Form a $5^1/_2$" long rope from clay by rolling on a hard surface. Shape head. Use the tip of a straight pin to scrape diamonds into body of snake. Shape curves into body. Refer to photograph. Bake clay following manufacturer's directions. Allow to cool thoroughly.

### Step Ten:

Using a paintbrush, paint horseshoes and finishing nail with black gloss acrylic enamel. Allow to dry thoroughly.

### Step Eleven:

Wind turntable onto musical movement. Using industrial-strength glue, glue two bales of hay to center of plaque. Stack remaining bales on top and glue into place. Allow to dry thoroughly.

### Step Twelve:

Make a lasso by wrapping cotton rope into a circle and secure with knots. Glue lasso to saddle and glue saddle on top of hay bales. Glue on horseshoes, cowboy hat, cowboy boots, cow skull, pitchfork, dogs, snake, barrel, and wagon wheel, referring to photographs for placement or place as desired. Allow to dry thoroughly.

### Step Thirteen:

Unwind turntable from base. Carefully hammer finishing nail into center of horseshoes. Wind turntable back onto base.

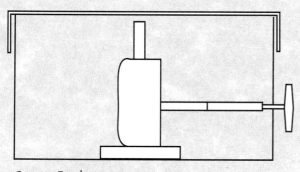

*Country Roads Diagram*

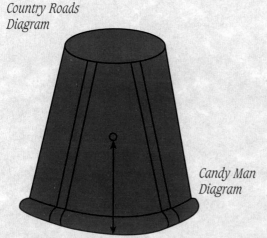

*Candy Man Diagram*

# Candy Man

## Materials Needed

### For the Base, Including Music Box Accessories:
King-size gumball machine and stand
18-note key-wind musical movement
Key extender, $1^1/_2$"
T-bar winding key, $^3/_4$"

### Decorative Accessories for Music Box Pictured:
Large gumballs, approximately 4 pounds

### Adhesive:
Epoxy

### Tools:
Drill with $^1/_4$" drill bit

## Step-by-Step Assembly

### Step One:
Disassemble gumball machine following manufacturer's directions.

### Step Two:
Mark the hole at center of back $4^1/_8$" from bottom. Drill a $^1/_4$" hole, referring to diagram at left.

### Step Three:
Turn base upside down. Wind key extender onto musical movement. Place musical movement inside base. Wind winding key onto key extender from the outside, making sure winding-key shaft is centered in hole.

### Step Four:
Mix epoxy following manufacturer's directions. With the base upside down, glue musical movement to the flat metal plate inside gumball machine. Allow to dry thoroughly upside down.

### Step Five:
Reassemble gumball machine and assemble stand. Attach gumball machine to stand and fill with gumballs.

# Candy Man

# Around the World

## Materials Needed

### For the Base, Including Music Box Accessories:
Unfinished recipe box,
   5³/₄" wide x 3³/₄" deep x 4" high
18-note key-wind musical movement
T-bar winding key, ³/₄"
Découpage
Sandpaper
Wood sealer

### Decorative Accessories for Music Box Pictured:
Assortment of stamps
Greeting card or postcard with traveling photo
2 brown ultra-suede strips, ¹/₂" wide x 16¹/₂" long
2 buckles, ¹/₂"
4 brass corner brackets, ⁵/₈"
Hasp catch, 1³/₄" x ⁵/₈"
Small padlock

### Acrylic Paint Color:
Blue-gray

### Adhesives and Spray Sealer:
Industrial-strength glue
Tacky glue
Gloss spray sealer

### Tools and Brushes:
Drill with ¹/₄" drill bit
Hammer
Old paintbrushes
Paintbrush
Ruler
Scissors
X-acto knife

## Step-by-Step Assembly

### Step One:
Using sandpaper, sand box. Refer to instructions for Sanding on page 14. Using an old paintbrush, apply wood sealer to box following manufacturer's directions. Allow to dry thoroughly.

### Step Two:
Using a paintbrush, paint box inside and outside with blue-gray acrylic paint. Refer to instructions for Painting on page 14. Spray with gloss sealer.

### Step Three:
Using an old paintbrush, apply a thin layer of découpage to box and sides of lid, working an area about 3" square at a time. Place stamps on box and lid sides, overlapping them as desired. Stamps should be placed over opening between lid and box — it will be cut open later. Using a ruler and an X-acto knife, cut greeting card to fit top of box. Apply a thin coat of découpage to lid top and place card in position. Refer to instructions for Découpaging on page 12.

### Step Four:
Using an old paintbrush, apply a thin layer of Tacky glue to wrong side of one ultra-suede strip. Starting at bottom front left corner, ³/₄" in from side and 1¹/₂" from bottom, press strip to box, wrapping it around bottom, back, top, and front of box. Slide a buckle on and make a small hole to accommodate the stem of the buckle at center 1" from the end. Using scissors, cut corners of ultra-suede strip on a 45° angle. Repeat process for remaining ultra-suede strip on other side of box. Allow to dry thoroughly.

### Step Five:
Using the X-acto knife, carefully cut opening between box and lid, starting at the back.

### Step Six:
Drill a ¹/₄" hole at center back of box ³/₄" from bottom. Using industrial-strength glue, glue musical movement inside box, making sure winding-key shaft is centered in hole. Allow to dry thoroughly.

### Step Seven:
Carefully hammer corner brackets on box. Turn the box back-side down, center hasp catch, and carefully hammer in nails. Put padlock on hasp catch, and wind on winding key. Fill box with favorite vacation photos.

# Chariots of Fire

## Materials Needed

### For the Base, Including Music Box Accessories:
Frisbee, 8$^{1}/_{2}$" diameter
Plywood circle, 3" diameter x $^{1}/_{8}$" thick
18-note key-wind musical movement
Metal turntable, 1$^{3}/_{4}$"
Sandpaper

### Decorative Accessories for Music Box Pictured:
Gold-tone plastic trophy cup, 4"
Sports equipment (plastic, wooden, or ceramic):
> Baseball
> Basketball
> Bowling ball
> Bowling pin
> Football
> Golf bag
> Skis
> Soccer ball
> Tennis racket
> Etc.

### Adhesive:
Industrial-strength glue

## Step-by-Step Assembly

### Step One:
Turn frisbee upside down. Using sandpaper, rough up plastic on center inside of frisbee.

### Step Two:
Using a generous amount of industrial-strength glue, glue plywood circle to sanded section of frisbee. Allow to dry thoroughly.

### Step Three:
Wind metal turntable onto winding-key shaft. The turntable is the winding key. Apply glue to top of musical movement, and press onto plywood circle so turntable is centered. Carefully wind turntable and turn frisbee over while music is playing. While rotating, make sure frisbee is turning even and level. Adjust as necessary. Allow to dry thoroughly.

### Step Four:
Using industrial-strength glue, glue trophy cup to center top of frisbee. Allow to dry thoroughly.

### Step Five:
Glue three or four larger pieces of sports equipment around trophy cup — close to or leaning on. Allow to dry thoroughly. Stack a few more pieces of sports equipment, filling in bare areas, and glue in place. Allow to dry thoroughly. Do not try to glue on too many pieces at once, or they could shift and slide while drying. Repeat until all pieces of sports equipment have been used.

## Music Box Variations

- This music box can be made into one for either a male or a female. Using the materials list and assembly instructions, assemble as instructed. Frisbees are available in a number of different colors — including neon and "glow-in-the dark." This music box makes a wonderful gift for any sports fanatic, including team members and coaches.

- Another fun idea would be to use an old 45 r.p.m. record or a compact disc as the base, instead of a frisbee. Simply glue a clear tone musical movement to one side of record or disc, winding-key shaft side pointing up. When dry, wind turntable onto winding-key shaft. Decorative accessories might include miniature musical instruments, such as a piano, clarinet, saxophone, trumpet, violin, flute, guitar, and drums. A bow tied from ribbon that resembles "music" would add character. For the song, choose one of these favorites:

  - Music, Music, Music
  - The Entertainer
  - Sound of Music
  - I'd Like to Teach the World to Sing
  - I Write the Songs

## Materials Needed

### For the Base, Including Music Box Accessories:
Round chipboard box, 2" high x 4¹/₂" diameter
Round wooden plaque, 4" diameter x ¹/₄" thick
18-note key-wind musical movement
Turntable, 3"
Sandpaper

### Decorative Accessories for Music Box Pictured:
3 wooden apples, (2) ¹/₂", (1) ³/₄"
Wooden bell, 1"
3 wooden books, (1) 1¹/₄", (1) 1¹/₂", (1) 1³/₄"
3 wooden blocks, ³/₈"
Round toothpicks
Chalkboard, 2" x 4"
Thin wire, 5"
Teddy bear, 2¹/₂"
Miniature spelling test
School desk, 1³/₄"
Small amount of gray sculpting clay
Small amount of green sculpting clay
Flag-print fabric, 2¹/₂" x 4¹/₂"
Gray embroidery floss, 8"
Yellow ruler-print ribbon, 15"

### Acrylic Paint Colors and Stain:
Black
Brown
Green
Metallic gold
Off-white
Pink
Red
Yellow
American walnut stain

### Adhesives and Spray Sealers:
Hot glue sticks
Industrial-strength glue
Tacky glue
Gloss spray sealer
Matte spray sealer

### Tools and Brushes:
Drill with ¹/₄" drill bit
Glue gun
Iron
Old paintbrush
Paintbrushes
Paper towels
Straight pin

## Step-by-Step Assembly

### Step One:
Prepare chipboard box. Refer to instructions for Preparing Boxes on page 14.

### Step Two:
Using a paintbrush, paint box and apples with red acrylic paint. Paint bell with metallic gold and bell's handle with brown. Paint books and blocks, referring to photograph for paint colors or paint as desired. Cut a ¹/₄" length from the end of a round toothpick to make a piece of chalk. Paint it with off-white. Using a small paintbrush, paint letters and words on blocks and books. Refer to instructions for Painting on page 14. Spray with gloss sealer.

### Step Three:
Using sandpaper, sand plaque and edges of chalkboard. Refer to instructions for Sanding on page 14. Using an old paintbrush, stain plaque and edges of chalkboard. Refer to instructions for Staining on pages 15-16. Spray with gloss sealer.

### Step Four:
Using gray sculpting clay, sculpt a mouse. Knead and form a small ball from clay. Shape it so it looks like an egg half with one pointed end, about ⁵/₈" long. Use the tip of a straight pin to scratch small lines on body to resemble hair. Roll two small balls of clay and flatten for ears. Press ears onto mouse. Using green sculpting clay, sculpt leaves — two for large apple and one for each small apple. Roll small balls of clay and

flatten. Pinch one side to give shape to the leaves. Use the tip of a straight pin to scratch veins in leaves. Bake clay following manufacturer's directions. Allow to cool thoroughly.

### Step Five:

Using a small paintbrush, paint the eyes and nose on mouse with black, and wash inside ears with pink. Cut small lengths from a round toothpick to make apple stems. Glue stems inside apples. Paint them with brown. Using industrial-strength glue, glue leaves on apples. Dry-brush leaves with brown. Refer to instructions for Dry Brushing on page 13. Cut a 1" length from the end of a round toothpick to make a pencil. Paint it with red, yellow, and black to resemble a pencil. Spray all painted pieces with gloss sealer.

### Step Six:

Drill a ¼" hole in center of lid on box. Using industrial-strength glue, glue musical movement to inside of lid, making sure winding-key shaft is centered in hole. Centering turntable, glue it to bottom of plaque. Allow to dry thoroughly.

### Step Seven:

Using chalkboard as pattern, cut flag-print fabric ¼" larger around all sides. Press edges under ¼", and, using Tacky glue, glue flag to back side of chalkboard. Glue lid on box. Draw words, math problem, and girl on chalkboard. Refer to photograph. Paint with off-white. Spray with matte sealer.

### Step Eight:

Bend thin wire into shape of glasses, making sure size is appropriate to fit on school desk. Paint with metallic gold. Spray with gloss sealer.

### Step Nine:

Wind turntable onto musical movement. Glue chalkboard in upright position, centering on plaque. The turntable is the winding key. On flag side, glue on teddy bear, large apple, blocks, and bell. Glue spelling test to teddy bear. On painted side of chalkboard, glue on desk, books, apples, pencil, glasses, and chalk. Refer to photographs. Glue one end of gray floss to underside of mouse for tail. Glue mouse to top of chalkboard, winding tail down the side. Using Tacky glue, glue ruler-print ribbon around box.

 *Funeral March of the Marionettes*

# Materials Needed

## For the Base, Including Music Box Accessories:
Oval sign plaque, 8" x 13½" x ⅝" thick
18-note key-wind double-action
    musical movement
Key extender, ½"
T-bar winding key, ¾"
Sandpaper
Wood sealer

## Decorative Accessories for Music Box Pictured:
Brass planter, 3" high x 4½" diameter
Wooden egg, 3½"
2 wooden paint pallets, 2"
Wooden heart, ½"
Wooden double heart, 1¾"
Muslin doll body, 15"
Straw hat, 3½"
Black cat, 3"
3 black flying bats with 2½" wingspan
Witch hat, 4"
Black soft-sculpture spider, 3"
Small spring, 5½"
5 two-ounce packages of orange sculpting clay
½ of two-ounce package of green sculpting clay
Wooden dowel, ⁵⁄₁₆" diameter x 4½" length
Balsa wood, 2½" x ¼" x ⅛" thick
Purple Halloween-print fabric, ¼ yard
Black-and-orange striped-print fabric, ¼ yard
Narrow elastic, 1 yard
Matching thread
Gray thread
Gray wavy wool doll hair, 6"

## Acrylic Paint Colors, Acrylic Enamel Paint, Antiquing Gel, Primer, and Fabric-Painting Medium:
Black
Bright green
Brown
Dark gray
Dark purple
Medium purple
White
Yellow
Black gloss acrylic enamel
Brown antiquing gel
Primer
Fabric-painting medium

## Adhesives and Spray Sealers:
Hot glue sticks
Industrial-strength glue
Tacky glue
Gloss spray sealer
Matte spray sealer

## Tools, Brushes, and Sponges:
Drill with ¼" and ⁵⁄₁₆" drill bits
Fine-point permanent black marker
Glue gun
Natural sponge
Old clean rag
Old paintbrushes
Paintbrushes
Paper towels
Pinking shears
Ruler
Screwdriver
Sewing machine
Soft-sculpture needle, 5"
Straight pins
Wire cutters

# Step-by-Step Assembly

### Step One:
Using primer, spray brass planter. Allow to dry thoroughly.

### Step Two:
Using sandpaper, sand plaque. Refer to instructions for Sanding on page 14. Using an old paintbrush, apply wood sealer to plaque following manufacturer's directions. Allow to dry thoroughly.

### Step Three:

Using two packages of orange sculpting clay, sculpt pumpkins for legs. Divide each package in half, knead, and form four round balls from clay. Using a soft-sculpture needle, make indentations on clay balls. Refer to photograph. Position "pumpkin legs" under plaque, and apply slight pressure to top of plaque to slightly flatten pumpkins. Remove pumpkin legs from under plaque. To sculpt pumpkins that go on top of plaque, use $1^1/_2$ packages of clay for largest pumpkin, 1 package for medium-sized pumpkin, and $^1/_2$ package for smallest pumpkin. Sculpt pumpkins by repeating the same process for sculpting the pumpkin legs. Using the soft-sculpture needle, make a small hole in the center top of each of these three pumpkins. Using green sculpting clay, sculpt three small stems. Place stems in holes. Sculpt leaves by rolling small amounts of green clay into small balls and slightly flatten. Pinch one side to give shape to the leaves. Use the needle to scratch veins in leaves. Carefully press leaves onto pumpkins. To make vines, roll small amounts of green clay on a hard surface to form a rope. Wrap and loop vines around tops of pumpkins. Refer to photograph. Bake clay following manufacturer's directions. Allow to cool thoroughly.

### Step Four:

Using a paintbrush, paint brass planter for witch's pot, wooden egg for crow's body, pallets for crow's wings, plaque, dowel, and balsa wood with black acrylic paint. Paint $^1/_2$" heart for crow's beak and double heart for crow's feet with yellow. Refer to instructions for Painting on page 14.

### Step Five:

Using wire cutters, cut three pieces of spring: one $1^1/_4$" length, one $1^3/_4$" length, and one $2^1/_4$" length. Using a glue gun, hot-glue springs to the three plastic disks that are on top of double-action musical movement turntable. Paint springs, disks, and top of turntable with black gloss acrylic enamel. Allow to dry thoroughly.

### Step Six:

Apply a small amount of dark gray acrylic paint to natural sponge. Sponge top of plaque. Refer to instructions for Sponging on page 15.

### Step Seven:

Using a paintbrush, paint the pumpkin stems with brown. Using an old paintbrush, antique all pumpkins with brown antiquing gel. Refer to instructions for Antiquing on page 12. Spray with gloss sealer.

### Step Eight:

Mix bright green acrylic paint and fabric-painting medium following manufacturer's directions. Using a paintbrush, paint the head and arms of muslin doll body. Mix black acrylic paint and fabric-painting medium following manufacturer's directions and paint doll's legs. Allow to dry thoroughly.

### Step Nine:

Using pinking shears, cut out a piece of Halloween-print fabric to measure $4^1/_2$" wide x 22" long for witch's skirt. Cut witch's shirt out of Halloween-print fabric, using bodice and sleeve patterns on page 83. Cut witch's pants out of black-and-orange striped-print fabric using pattern on page 83.

### Step Ten:

To make witch's pants, cut two pieces of elastic to fit snugly around witch's legs. Using a sewing machine and a narrow zig-zag stitch, sew elastic 1" from bottom edge of legs, stretching elastic as it is sewn. Place fabric pieces, right sides together. Sew a straight stitch seam along center front and center back seams. All seams are $^1/_4$", unless indicated otherwise. Clip curves. Place inside seams together with center seams matching. Sew along inseam. Fold waist over $^3/_8$", and sew a seam, leaving $^1/_2$" open to run elastic through. Cut a piece of elastic to fit snugly around witch's waist plus 2 inches. Run elastic through waist casing. Tie a double knot in the elastic, trim ends, and stitch opening closed.

### Step Eleven:

To make witch's shirt, place front and back bodice fabric pieces, right sides together. Sew shoulder seams. Cut two pieces of elastic to fit snugly around witch's arms. Using a sewing machine and a narrow zig-zag stitch, sew elastic $5/8$" from bottom edge of sleeve, stretching elastic as it is sewn. Gather top edge of sleeves. With right sides together, sew sleeves to bodice, adjusting gathers as necessary. With right sides together, sew under arms and side seams. Turn right side out.

### Step Twelve:

To make witch's skirt, using a sewing machine, sew a gathering stitch along one long edge of skirt piece. Gather so gathered seam measures approximately 10 inches. Using straight pins, pin skirt, right sides together, to bottom edge of bodice. Adjust gathers as necessary and sew together.

### Step Thirteen:

Transfer witch's face pattern on page 83 to doll body. Refer to instructions for Transferring on page 16. Using a paintbrush, paint eyes and cheeks, referring to pattern for paint colors. Allow to dry thoroughly. Paint white highlights in eyes. Using a permanent marker, outline eyes, cheeks, nose, mouth, and eyebrows.

### Step Fourteen:

Spray witch's head, arms, and legs with a light coat of matte sealer. Allow to dry thoroughly.

### Step Fifteen:

Using a paintbrush, paint eyes on crow's body, referring to photograph. Spray crow's body, all wood pieces, and witch's pot with gloss sealer.

### Step Sixteen:

Using industrial-strength glue, glue crow's feet, wings, beak, and hat to crow's body. Allow to dry thoroughly.

### Step Seventeen:

Drill holes in center bottom of witch's pot, using the template on page 83. Place musical movement into witch's pot, and secure it with screws, following manufacturer's directions.

### Step Eighteen:

To mark winding-key hole, wind key extender onto winding-key shaft. Paint a small dot of paint on the bottom of the key extender. Press witch's pot onto plaque so dot of paint marks placement for hole, and remove once hole has been marked. Refer to photograph for placement. Drill a $1/4$" hole, using paint dot as the center mark. Using industrial-strength glue, glue pumpkins, evenly spaced, to bottom of plaque for legs. Allow to dry thoroughly. Glue witch's pot to plaque, making sure key extender is centered in hole. Wind winding key onto key extender.

### Step Nineteen:

Drill a $5/16$" hole in plaque for crow's "perch," referring to photograph for placement. Glue dowel into $5/16$" hole, and, centering, glue balsa wood on top of dowel. Glue pumpkins and cat on plaque, referring to photograph for placement. Glue bats to tops of springs. Allow to dry thoroughly. (If bats cannot be found, they can be sculpted using black sculpting clay.)

### Step Twenty:

Dress doll (witch) in sewn clothes. Using a glue gun, hot-glue the back seam on shirt closed. Using gray thread, tie a few knots at center of wavy wool hair. Unravel each side. Glue knots to top of witch's head. Arrange hair and trim ends. Using pinking shears, cut two 1" squares from fabric scraps. Using Tacky glue, glue fabric squares to witch's hat. Using a glue gun, hot-glue witch's hat on her head and spider on brim of hat, referring to photograph for placement.

### Step Twenty-One:

Using industrial-strength glue, glue crow on perch and witch around witch's pot. Allow to dry thoroughly.

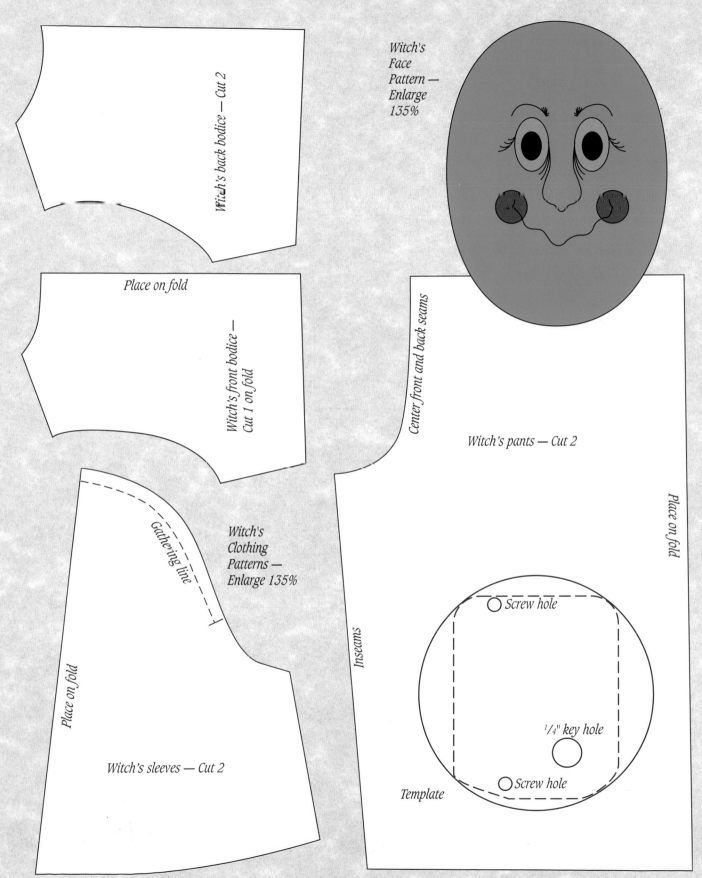

Witch's back bodice — Cut 2

Place on fold

Witch's front bodice — Cut 1 on fold

Witch's Face Pattern — Enlarge 135%

Center front and back seams

Witch's pants — Cut 2

Place on fold

Gathering line

Witch's Clothing Patterns — Enlarge 135%

Inseams

Place on fold

Witch's sleeves — Cut 2

Screw hole

1/4" key hole

Screw hole

Template

# How Great Thou Art

## Materials Needed

### For the Base, Including Music Box Accessories:
Oval wooden box, 2$^{1}/_{4}$" high x 28" circumference
18-note key-wind musical movement
Turntable, 1"
Key extender, 1$^{1}/_{2}$"
Sandpaper

### Decorative Accessories for Music Box Pictured:
Ceramic Amish boy sitting, 4$^{1}/_{2}$" high
Ceramic Amish girl standing, 7$^{3}/_{4}$" high
Metal pail, 2"
Styrofoam block, 2" x 2" x 2"
12 red apples, $^{1}/_{2}$"
Flower cart, 7$^{1}/_{2}$" x 3" x 2$^{1}/_{4}$"
Miniature cat figurine, 1$^{1}/_{2}$"
Miniature goose figurine, 1"
Quilt block fabric, 8" x 9"
Black cotton fabric, 8" x 9"
Fleece, 8" x 9"
Muslin, 6" x 7$^{1}/_{2}$"
Black extra-wide double-fold seam binding, 1 yard
Small amount of stuffing
Black thread
Off-white thread
Black quilting thread
2-ply jute, 12"
Tea dye or tea bags

### Acrylic Paint Colors, Acrylic Enamel Paint, and Stain:
Black
Dark brown
Dark country-blue
Green
Light Caucasian flesh-tone
Medium brown
Medium country-blue
Red
White
Black flat acrylic enamel
Light oak stain

### Adhesives and Spray Sealers:
Hot glue sticks
Industrial-strength glue
Tacky glue
Wood glue
Gloss spray sealer
Matte spray sealer

### Tools and Brushes:
Drill with $^{1}/_{4}$" drill bit
Glue gun
Needle
Old paintbrushes
Paintbrushes
Paper towels
Scissors
Sewing machine
Strong rubber band
X-acto knife

## Step-by-Step Assembly

### Step One:
Using sandpaper, sand box. Refer to instructions for Sanding on page 14. Using an old paintbrush, stain box. Refer to instructions for Staining on pages 15-16. Spray with matte sealer.

### Step Two:
Using a paintbrush, paint Amish figurines entirely with black acrylic paint. Refer to instructions for Painting on page 14. Dry-brush over face and hands with light flesh-tone, over clothing with dark and medium country-blue, over horse and buggy with medium brown, and over aprons and ruffles with white. Refer to instructions for Dry Brushing on page 13. Spray with matte sealer.

### Step Three:
To make quilt square, layer black cotton fabric right side down, fleece with quilt block fabric, right side up, on top. Using quilting thread, hand-quilt top. Using a sewing machine and black thread, sew seam binding around quilt block following manufacturer's directions.

### Step Four:

Tea-dye muslin. Refer to instructions for Tea Dyeing on page 16. When dry, cut into three 2$^1$/$_2$" x 6" strips using scissors. Fold each piece in half, right sides together, so there are three 2$^1$/$_2$" x 3" pieces. Using off-white thread, sew a $^1$/$_4$" seam on each 3" side. Turn right side out. Fill with stuffing to make sacks. Cut jute into three 4" lengths. Wrap one piece around each sack, and tie into a knot. Fray top edges.

### Step Five:

Using a paintbrush, paint pail with black flat acrylic enamel. Paint flower cart with dark brown acrylic paint and wheel with black. Dry-brush apples with red, leaves with green, and outer edges of leaves with brown. Allow to dry thoroughly. Spray flower cart and apples with gloss sealer.

### Step Six:

Place Amish figurines and cart on top of box, referring to photograph for placement. Remove Amish figurines. Place pail in back center of flower cart. Mark drill hole on cart at center under pail and remove pail. Drill a $^1$/$_4$" hole at mark. Mark another hole directly under hole in cart on top of lid. Remove cart and lid. Drill a $^1$/$_4$" hole at mark.

### Step Seven:

Using industrial-strength glue, glue musical movement to inside of lid, centering winding-key shaft in hole. Allow to dry thoroughly.

### Step Eight:

Using an X-acto knife, cut Styrofoam to fit in pail $^1$/$_4$" from top and place it in the pail. Using a glue gun, hot-glue Styrofoam in place. Glue apples on Styrofoam. Using industrial-strength glue, glue turntable to bottom of pail.

### Step Nine:

Using wood glue, glue lid on box. Using an old paintbrush, apply a thin layer of Tacky glue to the back side of quilt square. Place it on top of box, referring to photograph for placement. Using a strong rubber band, place it around the sides of box to hold down points on quilt square. Allow to dry thoroughly. When dry, remove rubber band.

### Step Ten:

Using scissors, cut a small hole in quilt square around winding-key shaft hole. Wind key extender onto winding-key shaft. Place flower cart on top. Place pail on cart with turntable winding shaft through hole. Wind turntable onto key extender. The turntable is the winding key. Checking the position of cart with Amish figurines on top, using industrial-strength glue, glue on top of quilt square. Glue sacks and cat figurine in cart and goose by Amish girl, referring to photograph for placement. Allow to dry thoroughly.

## Music Box Variations

- By using a larger box and larger quilt square, make this music box with more surface area to decorate. An Amish chapel would be a welcome addition to the scene!

- Use a quilt square with earth-tone colors. Turn this music box into a bountiful harvest one, complete with miniature Indian corn in the pail instead of apples. Sculpted pumpkins can be added to the top of the box, or added for legs. Refer to "Funeral March of the Marionettes" on page 81 for sculpting pumpkin legs.

- Try a barn on the top of the box, surrounded by a number of barnyard friends. Refer to the barn pattern for "Old MacDonald" on page 63, however, the barn will need to be enlarged to an appropriate size for the music box being created.

- A number of Amish figurines are available, including Amish women and girls quilting and Amish men and boys fishing.

# Up on the Housetop

## Materials Needed

### For the Base, Including Music Box Accessories:
Oval papier-mâché box,
   3" high x 25" circumference
Scrap of wood, 1½" x 2" x ½" thick
18-note key-wind musical movement
Left-hand threaded-shaft
Circular-motion rod, 4¾"
Key extender, ⅜"
T-bar winding key, ¾"
Textured snow

### Decorative Accessories for Music Box Pictured:
Hand-carved wooden house,
   4½" wide x 4" high x ½" thick
Christmas tree, 6"
2 wooden snowmen, (1) 1½", (1) 3"
2 prepainted plastic sleds, 2"
16 wooden gingerbread men, 1"
Prepainted Santa and sleigh with reindeer, 4"
1½"-wide scrap of red-and-green plaid fabric, 8"

### Acrylic Paint Colors:
Black
Brown
Country-blue
Gray
Off-white
Orange
Red
Tan
White

### Adhesives and Spray Sealers:
Industrial-strength glue
Tacky glue
Gloss spray sealer
Matte spray sealer

### Tools and Brushes:
Drill with ¼" drill bit
Metal cutters, if necessary
Old paintbrushes
Paintbrushes
Scissors

## Step-by-Step Assembly

### Step One:
Using a paintbrush, paint bottom and sides of papier-mâché box with red acrylic paint. Refer to instructions for Painting on page 14. Spray with gloss sealer.

### Step Two:
Using an old paintbrush, stain house with off-white, brown, country-blue, gray, and black acrylic paints. Refer to photograph for stain colors or stain as desired. Refer to instructions for Staining on pages 15-16. Spray house with matte sealer.

### Step Three:
Using an old paintbrush, apply textured snow to entire box lid, Christmas tree, and housetop, following manufacturer's directions. Allow to dry thoroughly.

### Step Four:
Using a paintbrush, paint snowmen with white, hats with black, and gingerbread men with tan. Allow to dry thoroughly. Paint the faces and buttons on snowmen with black, the snowmen noses with orange, and the eyes, mouths, and buttons on gingerbread men with brown. Refer to photograph. Spray all pieces with gloss sealer.

### Step Five:
Cut scrap of plaid fabric into two ½"-wide strips. Fray edges and tie strips around snowmen's necks. Trim ends. Using Tacky glue, glue at knot. Refer to photograph.

### Step Six:
Set house on top of box 2" from back edge, referring to photograph for placement. Mark the hole that will accommodate the circular-motion rod 1" from rear center of house and 1" from edge of box. Drill a ¼" hole at the mark. Referring to diagram on page 89, drill a ¼" hole to accommodate winding key.

### Step Seven:

Push left-hand threaded-shaft into the accessory hole on side of musical movement. Wind key extender onto winding-key shaft. Using industrial-strength glue, glue scrap of wood into bottom of box and musical movement on top of scrap of wood, making sure left-hand threaded shaft is centered in hole in the top of the lid. Using Tacky glue, glue lid on box. Allow to dry thoroughly.

### Step Eight:

Using industrial-strength glue, glue house, Christmas tree, snowmen, and sleds to top of box, referring to photograph for placement. Glue gingerbread men, evenly spaced, around sides, aligning at bottom edge of box. Allow to dry thoroughly.

### Step Nine:

Bend the metal disk on circular-motion rod so that the disk is horizontal. Bend motion rod on a 70° angle. Glue bottom of sleigh to metal disk. If necessary, trim disk with metal cutters. Wind circular-motion rod onto left-hand threaded-shaft. Wind winding key onto key extender.

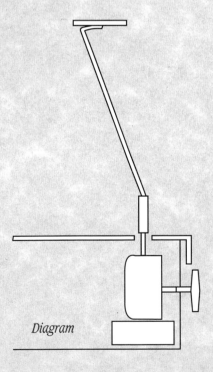

*Diagram*

## Music Box Variations

- This Christmas music box can simply be turned into a Halloween music box. Instead of having Santa and his reindeer flying over the housetop, have a witch on her broom flying overhead. The box can be painted with black and orange. Instead of gluing gingerbread men around the sides, glue on black plastic spiders or create a pattern using candy corn.

- Make this music box into a Wizard of Oz™ music box. Place the house so that a witch's legs are sticking out from underneath. Have a witch flying on a broom overhead. Paint the top of the box with a "yellow brick road" and, using Tacky glue and red glitter, cover the sides of the box. Additional Wizard of Oz™ figurines can be added as desired. Be sure to include Dorothy and Toto. The music for this music box might be: "Ding Dong, The Witch Is Dead."

- Instead of gluing gingerbread men to the side of the box, try painting one of the following patterns on the sides.

# Materials Needed

## For the Base, Including Music Box Accessories:
Medium tea box, 5" wide x 5" deep x 5" high
Styrofoam tree, 9"
18-note key-wind musical movement
Turntable, 1"
Sandpaper

## Decorative Accessories for Music Box Pictured:
2 wooden knobs, (1) $^3/_4$", (1) $2^1/_2$"
Wooden plug, $^3/_8$"
Wooden girl peg, 2"
3 wooden blocks, (1) $^3/_4$", (1) 1", (1) $1^1/_2$"
Wooden book, 2"
Wooden star, $2^3/_4$"
Wooden ball, $1^1/_4$"
Balsa wood, $2^1/_2$" x $^1/_2$" x $^1/_4$"
Balsa wood, $1^5/_8$" x $2^1/_4$" x $^1/_4$"
Santa glasses, $2^1/_4$"
Black plastic top hat, $^3/_4$"
Jingle bell, 20mm
Small spring, $^3/_4$" long
2 frosted pine sprays
Red wooden sled, $6^1/_2$" x $3^1/_2$"
Gold-tone horn, $3^1/_2$"
$^1/_2$ of two-ounce package of
    off-white sculpting clay
$^1/_2$ of two-ounce package of red sculpting clay
Scrap of blue and off-white checked cotton fabric
Red small-print cotton fabric, $^1/_4$ yard
Green plaid cotton fabric, $^1/_2$ yard
Off-white plush felt, 3" x 11"
Stuffing
Off-white upholstery thread
Thread to match fabrics
3-ply dark orange yarn, 1 yard
Cream wavy wool doll hair, 1 package
Dark red chenille, 1 yard
Thin gold ribbon, $1^1/_2$ yards
$^1/_2$"-wide red grosgrain ribbon, 5"
$^1/_4$"-wide green ribbon with gold hearts, 24"
$^1/_2$"-wide lace, $2^1/_2$"
Tea dye or tea bags

## Acrylic Paint Colors and Stain:
Black
Blue
Caucasian flesh-tone
Green
Ivory
Metallic gold
Purple
Red
Rose
Yellow
Walnut stain

## Adhesives and Spray Sealer:
Hot glue sticks
Industrial-strength glue
Mini hot-glue gold glitter stick
Tacky glue
Gloss spray sealer

## Tools, Brushes, and Sponges:
Drill with $^1/_4$" drill bit
Glue gun
Heavyweight cardboard, 3" square
Iron
Knife
Mini glue gun
Natural sponge
Needle
Old paintbrush
Paintbrush
Paper towels
Scissors
Sewing machine

# Step-by-Step Assembly

### Step One:
Place $2^1/_2$" knob flat-side down. Using industrial-strength glue, glue plug on knob for Santa's nose, centering from top to bottom. Allow to dry thoroughly.

### Step Two:

Tea-dye lace and blue, red, and green fabrics. Refer to instructions for Tea Dyeing on page 16.

### Step Three:

Using sandpaper, sand box and $2^{1}/_{2}$" x $^{1}/_{2}$" x $^{1}/_{4}$" piece of balsa wood. Refer to instructions for Sanding on page 14. Using an old paintbrush, stain box and sanded balsa wood. Refer to instructions for Staining on pages 15-16. Spray with gloss sealer.

### Step Four:

Using a paintbrush, paint $2^{1}/_{2}$" knob, $^{3}/_{4}$" knob, and girl peg head with flesh-tone acrylic paint. Paint small block with green, medium block with blue, and large block with purple. Paint $1^{5}/_{8}$" x $2^{1}/_{4}$" x $^{1}/_{4}$" piece of balsa wood with metallic gold. Paint book with green and pages on book with ivory. Paint star yellow. Refer to instructions for Painting on page 14.

### Step Five:

Apply a small amount of metallic gold acrylic paint to natural sponge. Sponge all sides of purple block. Refer to instructions for Sponging on page 15.

### Step Six:

Transfer doll face pattern on page 94 to girl peg (to make doll) and clown face pattern on page 94 to $^{3}/_{4}$" knob. Transfer clown box pattern to blue block. Refer to instructions for Transferring on page 16. Paint, referring to paint colors on pattern. Draw lines on ball and paint, referring to paint colors on pattern on page 94. Draw lines and dots on star, referring to pattern on page 94, and paint with green. Place glasses in position on $2^{1}/_{2}$" knob and mark eye placement. Remove glasses. Using the end of a paintbrush and black paint, dot $^{1}/_{4}$" eyes. Refer to photograph. Float nose and cheeks with rose. Spray all wooden pieces with gloss sealer.

### Step Seven:

Roll the off-white sculpting clay on a hard surface to make a 14"-long rope $^{1}/_{4}$" thick. Repeat with red sculpting clay. Hands must be washed. Carefully twist the two ropes together — red dye in clay easily smears onto off-white clay. Shape to form a candy

cane. Bake clay following manufacturer's directions. Allow to cool thoroughly. Spray with two to three coats of gloss sealer, letting each coat dry before applying the next.

### Step Eight:

Drill a $^{1}/_{4}$" hole in the center front of box. Using industrial-strength glue, glue stained balsa wood to back of box between hinges to secure lid in an open position. Glue musical movement inside box, making sure winding-key shaft is centered in hole. Glue turntable to center back of star and glue green block to flat side of $2^{1}/_{2}$" knob. The turntable is the winding key. Allow to dry thoroughly.

### Step Nine:

From the red fabric, cut out Santa's hat and mittens using the patterns on page 94. From the green fabric, cut one 7" x 14" piece and four $2^{3}/_{4}$" x $7^{1}/_{2}$" pieces.

### Step Ten:

Using a sewing machine, sew around mittens with matching thread, right sides together, using small stitches $^{3}/_{16}$" from edge, leaving straight edge open. Clip curves and between thumb and finger area. Turn and firmly fill with stuffing. Whip-stitch closed.

### Step Eleven:

Sew hat, right sides together, using a regular stitch and $^{1}/_{4}$" seam allowance. Using upholstery thread, hand-sew a gathering stitch between raw edge and very close to stitching. Refer to pattern on page 94. Pull gathers so gathered seam is $2^{1}/_{2}$" long. Tie a knot and cut thread.

### Step Twelve:

To sew arms, place $7^{1}/_{2}$" x $2^{3}/_{4}$" green fabric, right sides together, to make two sleeves. Sew a straight stitch along one long side of each sleeve and press open. Leaving sleeves open, place one sleeve on 7" x 14" fabric for body with right sides together. Refer to diagrams on page 94. Sew a $^{1}/_{4}$" seam along stitching line. Sew other sleeve to opposite side the same way. Fold sleeves outward. Fold in half, right sides together, so two 7" body sides are together.

Refer to diagrams on page 94. Sew a $1/4$" seam under arms and down sides. Using upholstery thread, hand-sew a gathering stitch along top of sleeve seam between raw edge and very close to stitching. Continue along body through one layer of fabric and along other sleeve. Pull gathers so gathered seam is $7^1/2$" long. Tie a knot and cut thread.

### Step Thirteen:

Using a knife, cut the top 3" off Styrofoam tree. Roll and press the cut edge of Styrofoam tree on a hard surface to round it off. With Santa's clothes still inside out, use a glue gun and hot-glue gathered area between sleeves to the top center of tree, making sure gathers are evenly spaced. Pull clothes down over tree and pull sleeves right sides out. Place a small amount of stuffing inside sleeves and around tree. Glue bottom $1/2$" edge of clothing to bottom of tree. Using industrial-strength glue, glue Santa's body into bottom of box — this might be a tight fit. Glue green block with "head" on top to center top of body. Allow to dry thoroughly.

### Step Fourteen:

Cut a small piece of blue fabric to fit around doll body. Apply a thin coat of Tacky glue to doll's body, and wrap fabric around it, pressing smooth. Glue lace around neck for collar. Allow to dry thoroughly.

### Step Fifteen:

Loosely wrap dark orange yarn around two fingers. Tie tightly at the center with upholstery thread, like making a pom-pom. Centering, hot-glue to top of clown head. Glue top hat to top of hair. Hand-sew a gathering stitch along one long edge of grosgrain ribbon. Pull gathers tightly. Tie a knot and trim. Using a mini glue gun with gold glitter stick, hot-glue ruffle to bottom of clown head. Glue spring to center top of blue block. Glue clown head on top of spring. Loosely wrap dark red chenille around two fingers. Tie tightly just off center, about $1/4$" from edge, with upholstery thread. Using a glue gun, hot-glue to top of doll's head, centered, with $1/4$" side for bangs. Tie a small bow from scrap of blue fabric. Glue in doll's hair.

### Step Sixteen:

Wrap wavy wool hair around cardboard square 15 times. Cut end. Using a small piece of upholstery thread, slide between cardboard and hair, and tightly tie a knot. Cut threads. Repeat until there are seven. Place a small amount of stuffing in hat. Using a glue gun, hot-glue hat to head, gathering fabric as needed. Glue one wavy wool hair piece under Santa's nose at the knot. Glue remaining six pieces, evenly spaced, around head. Back pieces should be next to hat. Using a 1-yard length of hair, glue along head for bangs by looping. Refer to photograph.

### Step Seventeen:

Slide mittens into sleeves and hot-glue in place. Cut one $3/4$" x 10" strip of plush felt to go around hat and two $3/4$" x 6" strips to go around cuffs. Wrap around hat and cuffs to check length and, if necessary, trim. Using Tacky glue, glue felt to fabric. Allow to dry thoroughly.

### Step Eighteen:

Tie ribbons around packages by wrapping gold ribbon around purple block, as if wrapping a present. Tie a "loopy" bow on top and trim ends. Wrap green and gold ribbon around gold piece of balsa wood. With the remaining green ribbon, tie a small bow, and, using a glue gun, hot-glue to package, referring to photograph. Sew jingle bell to tip of hat, and glue glasses on Santa's face.

### Step Nineteen:

Using industrial-strength glue, glue the following accessories in and on box, referring to photograph for placement or place as desired: pine sprays, candy cane, sled, presents, horn, doll, clown, ball, and book. Wind turntable onto winding-key shaft.

### Note:

The instructions and patterns for making a wooden sled, like the one in the photograph on page 90, are on page 95.

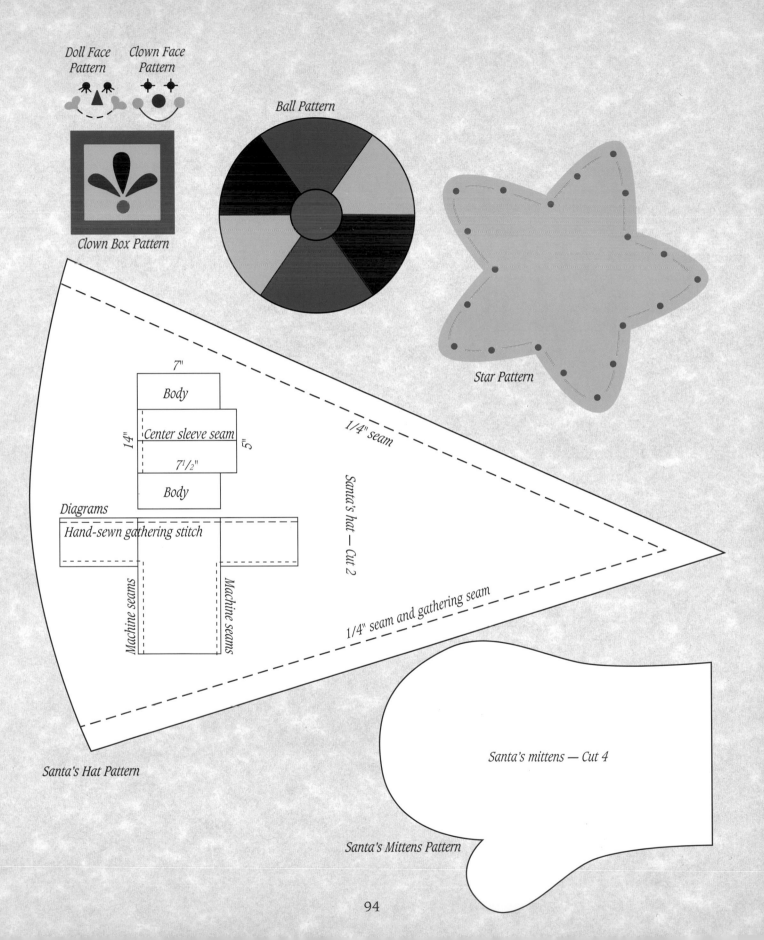

Doll Face
Pattern

Clown Face
Pattern

Ball Pattern

Clown Box Pattern

Star Pattern

7"

Body

14"  Center sleeve seam  5"

7¹/₂"

Body

Diagrams

Hand-sewn gathering stitch

1/4" seam

Santa's hat — Cut 2

Machine seams

Machine seams

1/4" seam and gathering seam

Santa's Hat Pattern

Santa's mittens — Cut 4

Santa's Mittens Pattern

# Wooden Sled

8 craft sticks
Bandsaw or scrollsaw
Glue gun
Drill with $1/8$" bit
Gold narrow cording, 12"

For the base of the sled, cut two craft sticks, each $3^1/4$" long, cutting off the rounded edges. Cut a notch the same width as the craft stick in each piece $1/2$" from each end, cutting halfway through craft sticks. For the runners, use two full-length craft sticks. Cut a notch the same width as the craft stick in each piece $1^1/2$" from one end and $2^3/8$" from the other end. Slide pieces together to form base of sled.

For the sides pieces on the top of the sled, use one craft stick. Mark the center of the craft stick and draw a line through the center at an angle. Cut along this line to make two pieces of equal length, leaving rounded edges on. Each piece should be $3^1/4$" long, measuring from rounded edge to point.

For the front piece on the top of the sled, cut one craft stick, $3^1/2$" long, using pattern for angled edges. Drill two $1/8$" holes in this piece to accommodate the cording.

Paint as desired with acrylic paint. Antique as desired with antiquing gel. Using a glue gun, hot-glue pieces together referring to patterns.

Slide gold cording through holes. Tie a knot at back of sled.

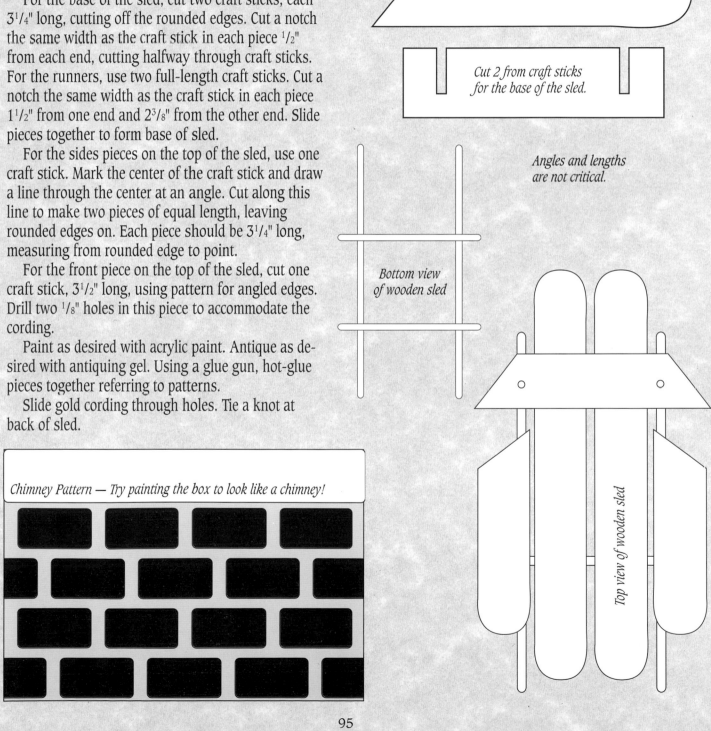

Wooden Sled Patterns

Cut 1 from craft stick.

Cut 2 from one craft stick.

Cut 2 from craft sticks for the base of the sled.

Angles and lengths are not critical.

Bottom view of wooden sled

Top view of wooden sled

Chimney Pattern — Try painting the box to look like a chimney!

95

# Silent Night

## Materials Needed

### For the Base, Including Music Box Accessories:
Ring box, 4½" wide x 4½" deep x 3½" high
Glass dome, 4½" high x 3" diameter
18-note key-wind miniature musical movement
Miniature T-bar winding key, ¾"
Textured snow
Sandpaper
Wood sealer

### Decorative Accessories for Music Box Pictured:
Miniature plastic nativity
Clear rhinestones, an assortment of sizes
Gold braid trim, 10"

### Acrylic Paint Colors, Glass Paint, and Antiquing Gel:
Black
Brilliant blue
Brown
Caucasian flesh-tone
Dark green
Light blue
Maroon
Metallic gold
Off-white
Purple
Metallic bright gold glass paint
Black antiquing gel

*North Star Pattern*

### Adhesives and Spray Sealer:
Industrial-strength glue
Tacky glue
Gloss spray sealer

### Tools, Brushes, and Sponges:
Drill with ³/₁₆" drill bit
Natural sponge
Old clean rag
Old paintbrushes
Paintbrushes
Paper towels
Tape

## Step-by-Step Assembly

### Step One:
Using sandpaper, sand box. Refer to instructions for Sanding on page 14. Using an old paintbrush, apply wood sealer to box following manufacturer's directions. Allow to dry thoroughly.

### Step Two:
Using a paintbrush, paint box and lid inside and out with brilliant blue acrylic paint. Refer to instructions for Painting on page 14.

### Step Three:
Apply a small amount of metallic bright gold glass paint to natural sponge. Sponge edges of box. Refer to instructions for Sponging on page 15. Spray with two to three coats of gloss sealer, letting each coat dry before applying the next.

### Step Four:
Using industrial-strength glue, glue rhinestones to box front. Refer to photograph for placement.

### Step Five:
Using a paintbrush, paint nativity pieces with black acrylic paint. Allow to dry thoroughly. Dry-brush faces with flesh-tone and remaining colors on nativity, referring to photograph on page 98 for paint colors or paint as desired. Refer to instructions for Dry Brushing on page 13. Spray with gloss sealer.

### Step Six:
Paint a small amount of off-white around bottom edge of glass dome. While paint is wet, press on center lid top. Wash paint off dome. Using an old paintbrush, apply textured snow to center of paint ring following manufacturer's directions. Allow to dry thoroughly.

### Step Seven:
Trace "North Star" pattern at left onto a small piece of paper. Tape paper to inside of dome, referring to photograph for placement. Using metallic bright gold glass paint, paint the star with two to three coats, letting each coat dry before applying the next. Paint a few small stars around the "North Star."

### Step Eight:

Using a paintbrush, paint the rhinestones with two or three coats of metallic bright gold glass paint. Allow to dry thoroughly.

### Step Nine:

Using a paintbrush, paint textured snow with off-white acrylic paint. Allow to dry thoroughly. Spray with gloss sealer.

### Step Ten:

Using industrial-strength glue, glue nativity pieces on lid top, referring to photograph below for placement. Glue angel to inside of dome. Allow to dry thoroughly.

### Step Eleven:

Glue glass dome on lid. Using Tacky glue, glue braid trim around base of dome. Allow to dry thoroughly.

### Step Twelve:

Using an old paintbrush, antique rhinestones with black antiquing gel. Refer to instructions for Antiquing on page 12. Spray with gloss sealer.

### Step Thirteen:

Drill a $^3/_{16}$" hole at back side of box base so miniature musical movement is centered. Using industrial-strength glue, glue musical movement to inside box on side, making sure winding-key shaft is centered in hole. Wind on miniature winding key. Place lid on top.

## Music Box Variations

- Try turning this music box into a Wizard of Oz™ music box. Substitute the miniature plastic nativity with Wizard of Oz™ figurines, placing the witch in the position that the angel occupies. Instead of painting the "North Star" on the glass dome, paint the message "Surrender Dorothy" or a rainbow in its place. Instead of painting the box and lid with acrylic paint and gluing the rhinestones to the box front, apply Tacky glue to box and lid and sprinkle with red glitter. Paint a "yellow brick road" instead of applying textured snow.

- Try turning this music box into a Frosty the Snowman music box. Substitute the miniature plastic nativity with a snowman figurine and several trees. Include a broom for Frosty! Instead of painting the "North Star" on the glass dome, paint several snowflakes. Refer to the snowflake patterns below.

Snowflake
Patterns

 *Parade of the Wooden Soldier*

## Materials Needed

### For the Base, Including Music Box Accessories:
Round papier-mâché drum,
    3" high x 5" diameter
Round wooden plaque,
    $4^{1}/_{2}$" diameter x $^{3}/_{8}$" thick
18-note key-wind musical movement
Turntable, $2^{1}/_{2}$"
Sandpaper
Wood sealer

### Decorative Accessories for Music Box Pictured:
6 prepainted wooden nutcrackers,
    (3) 5", (3) $2^{5}/_{8}$"

### Acrylic Paint Colors:
Blue
Metallic gold
Red

### Adhesive and Spray Sealer:
Industrial-strength glue
Gloss spray sealer

### Tools and Brushes:
Drill with $^{1}/_{4}$" drill bit
Old paintbrush
Paintbrushes

## Step-by-Step Assembly

### Step One:
Using a paintbrush, paint papier-mâché drum with red, blue, and metallic gold acrylic paints, referring to photograph for paint colors. Refer to instructions for Painting on page 14. Spray with gloss sealer.

### Step Two:
Using sandpaper, sand plaque. Refer to instructions for Sanding on page 14. Using an old paintbrush, apply wood sealer to plaque following manufacturer's directions. Allow to dry thoroughly. Using a paintbrush, paint plaque with red and edges with metallic gold. Spray with gloss sealer.

### Step Three:
Drill a $^{1}/_{4}$" hole in center of drum top to accommodate winding-key shaft.

### Step Four:
Using industrial-strength glue, glue musical movement to inside of drum top, centering winding-key shaft in hole. Allow to dry thoroughly.

### Step Five:
Glue turntable to center of bottom side of plaque. Allow to dry thoroughly.

### Step Six:
Wind turntable onto musical movement. Glue the 5" nutcrackers, evenly spaced, $^{1}/_{2}$" from edge of plaque. The turntable is the winding key. Glue the $2^{5}/_{8}$" nutcrackers, evenly spaced, between the 5" nutcrackers. Refer to photograph. Allow to dry thoroughly.

## Music Box Variations

- Use figurines of "the three kings." Acrylic paint colors can be changed to coordinate with the color scheme of the kings. The appropriate song for this music box would be "We Three Kings."

- Use snowmen figurines. Acrylic paint colors can be changed to coordinate with the color scheme of the snowmen. Song titles for this music box could be "Let It Snow" or "Frosty the Snowman."

- A drummer boy figurine might be placed on the top center of the papier-mâché drum. The appropriate song for this music box would be "The Little Drummer Boy."

- A castle figurine could be placed on the top, center of the papier-mâché drum. Textured snow can be applied to top of drum. The appropriate song for this music box would be "Winter Wonderland."

## Materials Needed

### For the Base, Including Music Box Accessories:
Hexagon papier-mâché box lid,
    $1^1/_4$" high x $23^1/_2$" circumference
Basswood, 4" x 16" x $^1/_4$" thick
20 basswood sticks, $^1/_8$" high x $^1/_8$" thick x 24" long
18-note key-wind musical movement
Turntable, $^1/_2$"
6 wooden knobs, $1^1/_4$"
Sandpaper

### Decorative Accessories for Music Box Pictured:
3 doll house windows (8-light),
    $2^9/_{16}$" wide x $5^1/_{16}$" high
Prepainted cat family figurines (resin or ceramic),
    $1^1/_8$" to $3^1/_4$" high (tree and fireplace required)
6 prepainted resin wreaths, $1^1/_4$"
Dark blue with gold snowflake
    cotton fabric, $^1/_8$ yard
Lightweight cardboard, 5" x 17"
Evergreen rug yarn, 70"
Mauve rug yarn, 70"
Rose rug yarn, 70"
Invisible thread

### Acrylic Paint Colors and Antiquing Gel:
Bright red
Green
Metallic gold
Off-white
Brown antiquing gel

### Adhesives and Spray Sealer:
Industrial-strength glue
Tacky glue, thin-bodied
Wood glue
Gloss spray sealer

### Tools and Brushes:
Drill with $^1/_2$" drill bit
Needle
Newspaper
Old clean rag
Old paintbrushes
Old toothbrush
Paintbrush
Saw
Scissors
X-acto knife

## Step-by-Step Assembly

### Step One:
Using a saw, cut 4" x 16" piece of basswood into two 4" x 8" pieces. Using wood glue, glue sides together to make an 8" x 8" square. Allow to dry thoroughly. Cut basswood sticks into 8" long sticks. Using an X-acto knife, randomly cut "V" notches in 8" long basswood sticks to resemble hardwood floor planks.

### Step Two:
To make hardwood floor, apply a thin layer of wood glue to one side of 8" basswood square. Place sticks on top with long sides touching, making sure "V" notched sides are facing up. Place a heavy book on top and allow to dry thoroughly.

### Step Three:
Using an old paintbrush, antique all figurines and resin wreaths with brown antiquing gel. Refer to instructions for Antiquing on page 12. Spray with gloss sealer.

### Step Four:
Using scissors, cut two 17" strips from cotton fabric. Using thin-bodied Tacky glue, laminate one piece to each side of cardboard. Refer to instructions for Laminating on page 13.

### Step Five:
When hardwood floor has thoroughly dried, place it, right side down, and center the papier-mâché box lid, open end down, on hardwood floor. Draw a line around it. Using a saw, cut out hexagon hardwood floor. Cut the bottom short edges off windows so they will sit flat and straight. Using sandpaper, sand top and sides of hardwood floor and windows. Refer to instructions for Sanding on page 14.

### Step Six:

Using a paintbrush, paint outside of papier-mâché box lid with bright red acrylic paint. Paint knobs with metallic gold. Refer to instructions for Painting on page 14.

### Step Seven:

Cover working area with newspaper. To "spatter" lid, dip the bristles of an old toothbrush into "thinned" green paint. Holding toothbrush a few inches away from the lid, run thumb across bristles. Spatter as much as desired. Wash out brush and repeat process with off-white. The size of spattering is determined by how much water is in the paint. Practice on newspaper before spattering lid. Allow to dry thoroughly. Spray with gloss sealer.

### Step Eight:

Using an old paintbrush, antique lid with brown antiquing gel. Using an old paintbrush, stain hardwood floor and windows with brown antiquing gel. Refer to instructions for Staining on pages 15-16. Spray with gloss sealer.

### Step Nine:

Using wood glue, glue windows to floor. Refer to photograph. Run a small bead of glue between each side of windows in the back. Allow to dry thoroughly. Using industrial-strength glue, glue knobs to top of lid at corners for legs. Allow to dry thoroughly.

### Step Ten:

To braid rug, handle all pieces of yarn as one. Tie an over-hand knot at center. Working with two strands of each color and starting at knot, braid until yarn is used. Measure 2" from knot, fold in half so it is flat. Using invisible thread, hand-sew together. Continue wrapping braid in an oval and tacking. Rug should have a 10" circumference when finished. Fold end under and tack in place. Trim excess.

### Step Eleven:

Arrange figurines and braided rug on top of hardwood floor, making sure as tree rotates it does not bump anything. Make a mark under center of tree. Remove figurines and braided rug. Drill a $1/2$" hole using mark as center. Using industrial-strength glue, glue musical movement to bottom of lid, making sure winding-key shaft is centered in hole. Glue turntable to the center bottom of tree. Allow to dry thoroughly.

### Step Twelve:

Cut three pieces of laminated cardboard to fit inside back of windows. Using an old paintbrush, apply a thin layer of thin-bodied Tacky glue to back of windows panes. Press laminated cardboard in windows.

### Step Thirteen:

Using industrial-strength glue, glue hardwood floor to lid (open end). Wind turntable onto winding-key shaft. The turntable is the winding key. Using thin-bodied Tacky glue, glue braided rug to front center of hardwood floor $3/8$" from front edge. Using industrial-strength glue, glue figurines to top and wreaths, spacing evenly, around sides of box lid. Allow to dry thoroughly.

## Music Box Variation

- A Halloween variation would be fun to try. Paint the box black and spatter it with orange and off-white. Black cotton fabric with stars would be a good substitute for the cotton fabric with snowflakes. Instead of cat family figurines, fireplace, and tree, use Halloween figurines. A witch's pot can be glued to the turntable using industrial-strength glue. Place it in the center of the hardwood floor. A witch figurine, and perhaps a couple of ghosts can be added. Braid the rug using black, orange, and off-white rug yarn. Make the rug round, large enough to go under the witch's pot and for a black cat to sit on. Spiders and cobwebs can be added over the windows. Instead of using wooden knobs for legs, sculpt six pumpkins. Refer to "Funeral March of the Marionettes" on page 81 for sculpting pumpkin legs.

# *When You Wish Upon A Star*

## Materials Needed

### For the Base, Including Music Box Accessories:
Treasure chest, $7^1/4$" wide x 5" deep x 3" high
Lightweight cardboard
Heavyweight cardboard
Balsa wood, 3" x 10" x $1/8$" thick
18-note key-wind musical movement
T-bar winding key, $3/4$"
4 wooden candle cups, 1"
Sandpaper
Steel wool
Wood sealer

### Decorative Accessories for Music Box Pictured:
Sun, 5" metal and wood ornament
Wooden half-moon, 3"
29 wooden stars, $3/4$"
Decorative latch, 1" high x $1^1/4$" wide
Brass sun charm
Brass moon charm
Bright blue fabric with gold stars, $1/4$ yard
Narrow gold braid trim, 1 yard

### Acrylic Paint Colors:
Brilliant blue
Metallic gold

### Adhesives and Spray Sealer:
Industrial-strength glue
Tacky glue
Gloss spray sealer

### Tools and Brushes:
Drill with $1/4$" drill bit
Hammer
Old paintbrush
Paintbrush
Ruler
Scissors
X-acto knife

## Step-by-Step Assembly

### Step One:
Using sandpaper, sand treasure chest. Refer to instructions for Sanding on page 14. Using an old paintbrush, apply wood sealer following manufacturer's directions. Allow to dry thoroughly.

### Step Two:
Using a paintbrush, paint treasure chest with brilliant blue acrylic paint, making sure to cover top inside edge of base and lid and inside edges about $1/2$" from top edge. A very smooth surface is required, apply at least three coats of acrylic paint, using steel wool to sand between each coat. Allow to dry thoroughly between each coat. Paint sun, half-moon, stars, and candle cups with metallic gold. Refer to instructions for Painting on page 14. Spray two coats of gloss sealer on treasure chest, inside and out, and all remaining painted pieces, letting each coat dry before applying the next. Allow to dry thoroughly.

### Step Three:
To line inside of treasure chest, lining supports will be needed. Using a ruler, measure length and width of inside of treasure chest. Add these measurements together and multiply by two. Using an X-acto knife, cut two strips from lightweight cardboard $1/2$" wide by the total length of measurement. One strip will be for the base and one will be for the lid. Score cardboard strips at corners. Using the same measurement plus one inch for length, cut two strips from fabric using scissors. Fabric width for base should equal the depth of base plus one inch. Fabric width for lid should equal the depth of lid plus one inch. Cut two fabric strips from fabric. Place fabric strips flat, wrong side down. Place cardboard lining supports $1/2$" from top edge of fabric strips and $1/2$" from left edge, scored side down. Starting with left $1/2$" edge, fold in $1/2$", and, using Tacky glue, glue fabric to cardboard. Then, fold top edge of fabric down $1/2$" and glue it to cardboard. Starting with right edge, glue supports into base and lid just below top edges. Allow to dry

thoroughly. Glue cut edge of fabric to bottom of base and to top of lid so fabric is tight against sides. Allow to dry thoroughly.

### Step Four:

Using the X-acto knife, cut two rectangles from heavyweight cardboard to fit inside bottom of base and top of lid. Using the cardboard as pattern plus one inch, cut two rectangles from fabric. Place fabric flat, wrong side down. Center cardboard on fabric. Fold edges over and glue to cardboard. Allow to dry thoroughly. Glue these pieces to bottom of base and to top of lid. Allow to dry thoroughly.

### Step Five:

To mark the hole position for winding-key shaft, place a dot of paint on winding-key shaft. Press musical movement, winding-key shaft side down, at back center of treasure chest inside base. Remove musical movement, and drill a $1/4$" hole in chest bottom, centering on paint dot. Using industrial-strength glue, glue musical movement inside box, making sure winding-key shaft is centered in hole.

### Step Six:

Using the X-acto knife, cut two $1 1/8$" high x 2" wide pieces (for sides), one $1 1/8$" high x $2 3/4$" wide piece (for front), and one 2" deep x $2 3/4$" wide piece (for top) from balsa wood. Using industrial-strength glue, glue side and front pieces together to make a cover for musical movement. Allow to dry thoroughly.

### Step Seven:

Cut one $1 3/4$" x 8" piece and one $2 3/4$" x $3 1/2$" piece from fabric. Using Tacky glue, glue the long strip of fabric around sides of balsa wood cover, centering and folding raw edges over. Glue remaining piece of fabric around balsa wood top. Glue top to sides of balsa wood cover. Refer to photograph. Glue fabric-covered balsa wood cover over musical movement. Refer to photograph.

### Step Eight:

Carefully hammer decorative latch to center front of treasure chest. Using industrial-strength glue, glue candle cups to bottom of treasure chest at corners for legs. Glue sun, half-moon, and stars, referring to photograph for placement.

### Step Nine:

Cut a 5" piece from gold braid trim. String sun and moon charms onto braid. Tie a knot 1" from both ends. Using remaining gold trim, tie a knot 1" from both ends. Make a bow by looping braid around fingers. Wrap 5" piece around center and tie a knot. Refer to photograph. Using Tacky glue, glue bow and charms to center back of fabric-covered balsa wood cover. Wind on winding key.

## Edelweiss

## Materials Needed

### For the Base, Including Music Box Accessories:
Oval brass planter with hollow pedestal
18-note key-wind musical movement
Key extenders, if necessary
T-bar winding key, $3/4$"

### Decorative Accessories for Music Box Pictured:
Potpourri

### Adhesive:
Industrial-strength glue

### Tools:
Drill with $1/4$" drill bit

## Step-by-Step Assembly

### Step One:
Drill a $1/4$" hole centered in brass planter bottom, making sure hole is centered in pedestal.

### Step Two:
Using industrial-strength glue, glue musical movement to inside bottom of brass planter, making sure winding-key shaft is centered in hole. Allow to dry thoroughly. Wind on winding key. If pedestal is very narrow, one or more key extenders can be added to make winding easier.

### Step Three:
Fill with potpourri.

*Pictured on page 108.*

# *Edelweiss*

# Camelot

## Materials Needed

### For the Base, Including Music Box Accessories:
Molding, 24" long x 2³/₄" high x ¹/₂" thick
Hardboard, 7" x 14" x ¹/₈" thick
18-note key-wind musical movement
Top-mount rotation assembly
Left-hand threaded turntable, 1"
Left-hand threaded-shaft extender, ³/₈"
Left-hand threaded-shaft extender, ¹/₂"
T-bar winding key, ³/₄"
8 faceted acrylic crystal balls, 1"
Coarse-grit sandpaper
Sandpaper
Steel wool

### Decorative Accessories for Music Box Pictured:
Pewter castle, 5" high
Pewter wizard, 3" high
3 additional pewter figurines, 1¹/₄" to 1¹/₂" high
8 long acrylic crystal drop prisms, 2"
Wooden dowels, assorted widths and lengths
Instant papier-mâché, 4 ounces
Scenic sand

### Acrylic Paint Colors, Spray Enamel Paint, and Primer:
Dark mossy green
Light mossy green
Black high-gloss spray enamel
Primer

### Adhesives and Spray Sealer:
Hot glue sticks
Industrial-strength glue
Tacky glue
Wood glue
Matte spray sealer

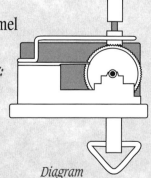

*Diagram*

### Tools and Brushes:
Drill with ¹/₄" and ¹/₂" drill bits
Glue gun
Old paintbrush
Paintbrush
Paper towels
Ruler
Saw
Strong rubber band

## Step-by-Step Assembly

### Step One:
Using a saw, cut eight 2¹/₄" pieces of molding on a 22¹/₂° angle. Refer to diagram on page 110. Using wood glue, glue molding together to form an octagon. Refer to diagram on page 110. Using a strong rubber band, place it around the sides of octagon to hold in place. Allow to dry thoroughly. When dry, remove rubber band.

### Step Two:
Using sandpaper, sand octagon. Refer to instructions for Sanding on page 14. Using primer, spray octagon. Allow to dry thoroughly.

### Step Three:
Place octagon on top of hardboard. Trace around the inside bottom to make box bottom. Turn octagon over and trace around the outside top to make box lid. Using a saw, cut bottom and lid from hardboard.

### Step Four:
Place hardboard box bottom in bottom of octagon box. Using a glue gun, hot-glue around inside edges of box bottom.

### Step Five:
A very smooth surface is required. Apply three coats of black high-gloss spray enamel to box, using steel wool to sand between each coat. Allow to dry thoroughly between each coat.

### Step Six:

Arrange pewter figurines on hardboard box lid. The center figurine will rotate. Refer to photograph for placement. Place dowel lengths under figurines to reach desired heights. Do not put a dowel under the center, rotating figurine. Remove figurines, and, using wood glue, glue dowels in place. Allow to dry thoroughly.

### Step Seven:

Mix instant papier-mâché following manufacturer's directions. Apply papier-mâché over entire hardboard lid surface and around dowels, sculpting ridges and peaks. Make holes in papier-mâché for the long acrylic crystal drop prisms by pushing them into the papier-mâché while it is wet. Remove and wash prisms — do not allow papier-mâché to dry on them. Refer to photograph. Allow to dry thoroughly.

### Step Eight:

Drill a $1/2$" hole in lid where rotating figurine will be to accommodate turntable shaft.

### Step Nine:

Using an old paintbrush, apply a thin layer of Tacky glue to top of papier-mâché surface and to lid sides. Sprinkle scenic sand in a smooth layer on top and sides. Allow to dry thoroughly and shake off excess sand.

### Step Ten:

Using a paintbrush, paint top and sides of lid with dark mossy green acrylic paint. Paint left-hand threaded turntable with dark mossy green. Refer to instructions for Painting on page 14. If rotating figurine is narrower than turntable, turntable will need to be cut down and sanded. Dry-brush lid with light mossy green. Refer to instructions for Dry Brushing on page 13. Spray box lid and turntable with matte sealer.

### Step Eleven:

Attach top-mount rotation assembly to musical movement following manufacturer's directions. Referring to diagram on page 109, wind left-hand threaded-shaft extenders onto top-mount rotation assembly. To mark winding-key hole, place musical movement inside box. It is very important that the left-hand threaded-shaft extenders are centered in the hole in the lid. Remove lid. Draw a line around musical movement. Remove musical movement, and paint a small dot of paint on the bottom of the winding-key shaft. Press musical movement back into box so dot of paint marks placement for hole, and remove once hole has been marked. Drill a $1/4$" hole, using paint dot as the center mark. Using industrial-strength glue, glue musical movement into box, making sure winding-key shaft is centered in hole. Glue lid on box, lining up hole in lid over left-hand threaded-shaft extenders. Allow to dry thoroughly.

### Step Twelve:

Using coarse-grit sandpaper, sand one side of each faceted acrylic crystal ball until it is flat. Sand off approximately $1/8$" to $1/4$". Place one ball under box at each corner. Sand until box is sturdy and level. Using industrial-strength glue, glue crystal balls to bottom of box at corners for legs. Allow to dry thoroughly.

### Step Thirteen:

Wind left-hand threaded turntable onto left-hand threaded-shaft extenders. Glue pewter figurines and long acrylic crystal drop prisms in place on top of lid and turntable. Allow to dry thoroughly. Wind on winding key.

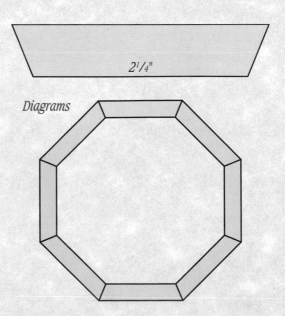

$2 1/4$"

*Diagrams*

# Camelot

# *Whistle While You Work*

## Materials Needed

### For the Base, Including Music Box Accessories:
Wooden trunk, 9" wide x 5$^1$/$_2$" deep x 5" high
18-note key-wind musical movement
Turntable, 1"
Key extender, $^1$/$_2$"
4 wooden bells, 1"
Sandpaper
Wood sealer

### Decorative Accessories for Music Box Pictured:
Assortment of Lego® building blocks
Yellow Lego® building board, 5" x 5$^1$/$_2$"
Border stencil, 1$^1$/$_4$"-wide design

### Acrylic Paint Colors:
To match Lego® building blocks:
  Blue
  Green
  Red
  Yellow

### Adhesives and Spray Sealer:
Industrial-strength glue
Stencil adhesive or tape
Gloss spray sealer

### Tools and Brushes:
Drill with $^1$/$_4$" drill bit
Old paintbrush
Paintbrush
Paper towels
Stenciling sponge brush

## Step-by-Step Assembly

### Step One:
Using sandpaper, sand trunk and lid. Refer to instructions for Sanding on page 14. Using an old paintbrush, apply wood sealer to trunk and lid following manufacturer's directions. Allow to dry thoroughly.

### Step Two:
Using a paintbrush, paint sides of trunk with yellow acrylic paint. Paint lid and bottom of base with blue and bells with red. Refer to instructions for Painting on page 14.

### Step Three:
Using stencil adhesive or tape, center border stencil between top and bottom of one side of trunk. Using a stenciling sponge brush, sponge the stencil with green, red, and blue acrylic paint. Dip a small edge of the sponge brush in green acrylic paint, stenciling one side at a time. Blot on paper towels. Lightly sponge one area, to be green, being careful not to get paint on unwanted areas. Allow to dry thoroughly. Carefully sponge over green areas again with enough coats to cover completely — do not apply paint too heavily or it will run under stencil. Do not remove stencil. Repeat process with red and then blue. When dry, remove stencil, and sponge the three remaining sides in the same way. Allow to dry thoroughly. Spray trunk, lid, and bells with gloss sealer.

### Step Four:
Drill a $^1$/$_4$" hole in center front of trunk.

### Step Five:
Using industrial-strength glue, glue a few Lego® blocks together for a winding knob. Glue turntable to back center of Lego® winding knob.

### Step Six:
Glue musical movement inside trunk, making sure winding-key shaft is centered in hole. Remove lid. Centering, glue 5" x 5$^1$/$_2$" yellow Lego® building board to top of lid. Turn trunk upside down, and glue one bell to bottom of box at corners for legs. Refer to photograph. Allow to dry thoroughly.

### Step Seven:
Wind turntable onto key extender. Wind key extender onto winding-key shaft. The turntable is the winding key. Using the remaining Lego® building blocks, create anything desired. Take the creation apart and build something new!

# *Happy Birthday*

## Materials Needed

### For the Base, Including Music Box Accessories:
Round chipboard box, 2" high x 4³/₄" diameter
18-note key-wind musical movement
Turntable, 1"
Wood sealer

### Decorative Accessories for Music Box Pictured:
Muslin bunny, 5"
Muslin pig, 5"
1¹/₂" prepainted resin birthday cake
2 wooden blocks, (1) ¹/₂", (1) ³/₄"
Wooden dowel, 1¹/₄" diameter x ¹/₂" length
White Battenburg doily, 4" square
Pink calico-print fabric, 4" x 15"
Lavender calico-print fabric, 4" x 13"
4mm green silk ribbon, 2 yards
4mm mauve silk ribbon, ¹/₂ yard
7mm pink silk ribbon, 25"
7mm purple silk ribbon, 2¹/₂ yards
Pink-and-gold flat ribbon, 18"
Narrow gold cording, 12"
Off-white quilting thread
Tea dye or tea bags

### Acrylic Paint Colors:
Dark green
Mauve
Plum
Yellow

*Lazy Daisy Pattern*

### Adhesives and Spray Sealer:
Hot glue sticks
Industrial-strength glue
Tacky glue
Gloss spray sealer

### Tools and Brushes:
Drill with ¹/₂" drill bit
Glue gun
Needle
Old paintbrushes
Paintbrush
Paper towels
Scissors

*French Knot Pattern*

## Step-by-Step Assembly

### Step One:
Prepare chipboard box. Refer to instructions for Preparing Boxes on page 14. Using an old paintbrush, apply wood sealer to box following manufacturer's directions. Allow to dry thoroughly.

### Step Two:
Using a paintbrush, paint box with plum acrylic paint. Paint ³/₄" block with mauve and ¹/₂" block with dark green. Paint dowel with yellow. Refer to instructions for Painting on page 14. Spray with gloss sealer.

### Step Three:
Tea-dye bunny, pig, and doily. Refer to instructions for Tea Dyeing on page 16.

### Step Four:
Pull a few of the loose threads on the long edges of pink and lavender calico-print fabric strips to fray edges. Fold fabric strips in half lengthwise, wrong sides together. Using quilting thread, hand-sew a gathering stitch ¹/₄" from frayed edges on fabric strips.

### Step Five:
Cut one 5" piece of purple silk ribbon and one 5" piece of pink silk ribbon to make straps for dresses. Fold purple silk ribbon in half to make a "V" shape. Using a glue gun, hot-glue it to the front center of bunny. Wrap ends over bunny's shoulders and hot-glue to back. Repeat process, using pink silk ribbon on pig. Tie a small bow from purple silk ribbon, and hot-glue it between bunny's ears. Cut a 6¹/₂" piece of pink silk ribbon. Wrap it around pig's head, and hot-glue to top of head, just off center. With remaining pink silk ribbon, tie a small bow at the center. Hot-glue on top of pig's head. Cascade ribbon tails, referring to photograph for placement, and hot-glue in place. Trim ends.

### Step Six:
Place bunny in a sitting position. Using a glue gun, place a small amount of hot glue between bunny's

legs and body so it will stay in a sitting position. Repeat process with pig.

### Step Seven:

Pull gathers tightly on lavender fabric strip. Wrap fabric around bunny, under arms, and tie a knot at back for bunny's dress. Tack dress in place with hot glue. Repeat process with pink fabric strip for pig's dress.

### Step Eight:

Using an old paintbrush, apply a thin layer of Tacky glue to top of lid. Centering, press doily on lid. Allow to dry thoroughly.

### Step Nine:

Thread remaining purple silk ribbon onto a needle and sew French knots approximately every $1^1/2$" (this will depend on pattern in ribbon) on pink-and-gold flat ribbon. Thread green silk ribbon onto a needle, and sew a Lazy Daisy stitch on each side of French knots. Refer to patterns on page 115 and refer to photograph below.

### Step Ten:

Drill a $^1/2$" hole at center front of lid 1" from front edge (seam is in back). Using industrial-strength glue, glue musical movement to inside lid, making sure winding-key shaft is centered in hole. Glue resin birthday cake to turntable. Allow to dry thoroughly.

### Step Eleven:

Using Tacky glue, glue lid on box, making sure seams on box and lid are aligned. Using industrial-strength glue, glue pink-and-gold flat ribbon around side of box, making sure seam is at center back. Glue dark green block on top of mauve block, and tie narrow gold cording around blocks for "presents," referring to photograph for placement. Wrap and glue a small piece of mauve silk ribbon around yellow dowel, top to bottom. Make a "loopy" bow, and glue to top of dowel.

### Step Twelve:

Wind turntable onto musical movement. The turntable is the winding key. Using industrial-strength glue, glue round "dowel" present in pig's hands and glue bunny, pig, and "block" presents to top of box, referring to photograph for placement.

## Music Box Variations

- It is simple to turn this music box into one to celebrate the birthday of a special someone turning "Sweet 16." Small porcelain dolls can be used instead of the bunny and the pig. Dress the dolls in "frilly" dresses. If a resin birthday cake with "16" candles cannot be found, sculpt one using sculpting clay in different colors.

- It is simple to turn this music box into a birthday reminder one might never forget! For all those celebrating birthdays "Over-the-Hill," this music box could be made by painting the chipboard box with black acrylic paint. For a special accent, spatter the sides of the box with white and silver acrylic paints. Refer to instructions for spattering on page 103. The figurines can hold black balloons.

- It is simple to turn this music box into a birthday music box for any baby ready to turn one year old. Paint the box with the appropriate colors for the sex of the child and decorate it with accessories fitting for a baby that age.

*Detail of stitching on ribbon shown.*

# *My Favorite Things*

# Materials Needed

### For the Base, Including Music Box Accessories:
Treasure chest, 7" wide x 4$^1/_2$" deep x 4" high
Hardboard, 6$^3/_8$" x 4" x $^1/_2$" thick
4 squares of balsa wood, 1$^3/_4$" x 1$^3/_4$" x $^1/_4$" thick
18-note key-wind musical movement
Turntable, 1"
Sandpaper

### Decorative Accessories for Music Box Pictured:
Patchwork teddy bear, 7"
Jointed short-haired teddy bear, 6"
Wired-body doll, 6"
Unfinished wooden rocking horse, 4$^1/_2$" x 6"
4 wooden blocks, $^3/_4$"
Wooden candle cup, 1$^1/_4$"
2 wooden knobs, (1) 1$^1/_4$", (1) 1$^3/_4$"
Wooden plug, $^3/_8$"
Wooden wheel, 2"
6 wooden buttons,
   (1) $^3/_8$", (1) $^1/_2$", (1) $^5/_8$", (1) $^7/_8$", (2) 1"
Wooden bead, $^1/_4$"
Square of wood, 1" x 1" x $^1/_8$" thick
Decorative brass lock, 1$^1/_4$" x 2"
Brass key charm, 1$^3/_4$"
Mirror, cut to fit inside lid
Wooden dowel, $^3/_{16}$" diameter x 2$^1/_2$" length
Wooden dowel, $^5/_{16}$" diameter x 2$^1/_4$" length
Gold-tone chain, 3"
2 small brass eye hooks
Brass button, $^1/_2$"
Brown ultra-suede, $^1/_8$ yard
36 hammered-brass upholstery nails
4mm dark red silk ribbon, 5"
4mm dark green silk ribbon, 6"
Navy-blue grosgrain ribbon, 9"
$^1/_2$"-wide lace, 12"
Ivory thread
Tea dye or tea bags

### Acrylic Paint Colors, Antiquing Gels, and Stain:
Black
Blue
Brown
Green
Metallic gold
Off-white
Orange
Purple
Red
Yellow
Black antiquing gel
Brown antiquing gel
American walnut stain

### Adhesives and Spray Sealer:
Industrial-strength glue
Super glue
Tacky glue, thin-bodied
Matte spray sealer

### Tools and Brushes:
Drill with $^3/_{16}$" and $^1/_4$" drill bits
Hammer
Needle
Old clean rag
Old paintbrushes
Paintbrushes
Paper towels
Pencil sharpener
Rotary cutter
Ruler
Scissors
Wire cutters, if necessary

# Step-by-Step Assembly

### Step One:
Using sandpaper, sand box. Refer to instructions for Sanding on page 14. Using an old paintbrush, stain box and 1" square of wood with stain. Using a paintbrush, stain rocking horse with brown, red, blue, black, and metallic gold acrylic paints, referring to photograph for paint colors or stain as desired. Refer to instructions for Staining on pages 15-16. Spray with matte sealer.

### Step Two:

Remove clothing from wired-body doll. Tea-dye clothes, lace, and patchwork teddy bear. Refer to instructions for Tea Dyeing on page 16.

### Step Three:

Using scissors, cut one piece of ultra-suede 7" x 4½". Set aside. Using ruler and rotary cutter, cut two long strips ⅝" wide. From these strips, cut four strips long enough to go from front top edge of chest bottom, around bottom, and up the back to the top edge of chest bottom. Refer to photograph. Cut one strip to go around top edge of chest bottom. Using an old paintbrush, apply a thin layer of thin-bodied Tacky glue to the back of ultra-suede strips. Press four short strips on first, then press remaining strip around top edge. Repeat with chest lid. Allow to dry thoroughly.

### Step Four:

Using a paintbrush, paint one block with red, one with yellow, one with green, and one with black. Paint ³⁄₁₆" dowel with black, candle cup with red, and 1¼" knob with off-white. Using a pencil sharpener, sharpen one end of ⁵⁄₁₆" dowel and sand. Paint dowel with yellow, plug with green, wheel with blue, 1¾" knob with green, and turntable sides with brown. Largest to smallest, paint buttons with purple, blue, green, red, orange, and yellow. Paint bead with off-white. Refer to instructions for Painting on page 14.

### Step Five:

Paint letters on blocks. Paint star and stripe on green knob. Paint gumball details on candle cup and off-white knob. Refer to patterns on page 120 for paint colors. Centering, paint a ⅛" line around side of wheel with yellow, and paint small red dots on yellow every ⅜".

### Step Six:

Using an old paintbrush, antique all painted wood pieces, except rocking horse, with brown antiquing gel. Antique brass lock and brass key with black antiquing gel. Refer to instructions for Antiquing on page 12. Spray all wood and brass pieces with matte sealer.

### Step Seven:

Drill a ³⁄₁₆" hole in bottom of candle cup and a ³⁄₁₆" hole in one side of black block. Using industrial-strength glue, glue one end of black dowel into block and one end into candle cup. Glue gumball knob on top of candle cup to make gumball machine. Glue plug to flat end of yellow dowel, and slide wheel onto dowel, gluing at center of dowel to make top. Glue green knob onto turntable. Glue purple button to center of 1" stained square of wood. Continue gluing and stacking on top of each other, largest to smallest, with off-white bead on top to make stack toy. Allow to dry thoroughly.

### Step Eight:

Hammer upholstery nails in chest, referring to photograph for placement. If upholstery nails are too long, trim with wire cutters. Hammer brass lock to front of chest.

### Step Nine:

Using industrial-strength glue, glue squares of balsa wood inside chest. Glue one piece to each side, inside chest, centering from side to side, with bottom edge touching bottom of chest. The hardboard will rest on these. Glue mirror to inside of lid. Allow to dry thoroughly.

### Step Ten:

Drill a ¼" hole in front right-hand corner of hardboard ⅞" from each edge. Trim 7" x 4½" piece of ultra-suede to size of hardboard. Using thin-bodied Tacky glue, laminate ultra-suede to top of hardboard, cutting fabric around drilled hole. Refer to instructions for Laminating on page 13.

### Step Eleven:

Using industrial-strength glue, glue musical movement to bottom side on hardboard, making sure winding-key shaft is centered in hole. Allow to dry thoroughly.

### Step Twelve:

Re-dress doll. Make one rosette with dark red silk ribbon. Refer to instructions on page 25. Hand-sew rosette to center of neck on doll's dress. Using ivory thread, hand-sew a gathering stitch along straight edge of lace. Pull gathers. Wrap lace around patch-work bear's neck, tack, and sew brass button to center front over the lace. Tie a small bow with navy-blue grosgrain ribbon, and glue it under jointed teddy bear's chin. Trim ends. Tie dark green silk ribbon to key and around rocking horse's neck.

## Step Thirteen:

Using industrial-strength glue, glue hardboard in chest, resting on squares of balsa wood, making sure drilled hole is in right front corner. Attach chain from lid to chest on left-hand side, using eye hooks. Apply a small amount of super glue to hinges so lid cannot close.

## Step Fourteen:

Wind turntable onto winding-key shaft. The turntable is the winding key. Using industrial-strength glue, glue rocking horse, teddy bears, and gumball machine into chest, referring to photograph for placement. Allow to dry thoroughly. Glue doll, blocks, stack toy, and top in box. Allow to dry thoroughly.

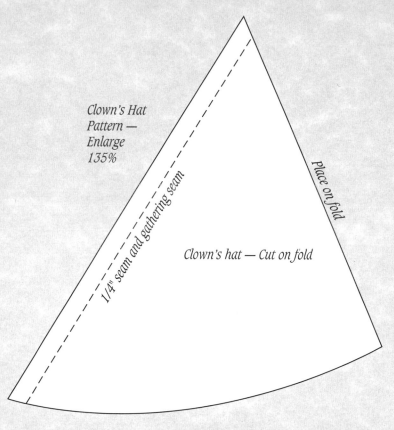

Clown's Hat Pattern — Enlarge 135%

1/4" seam and gathering seam

Place on fold

Clown's hat — Cut on fold

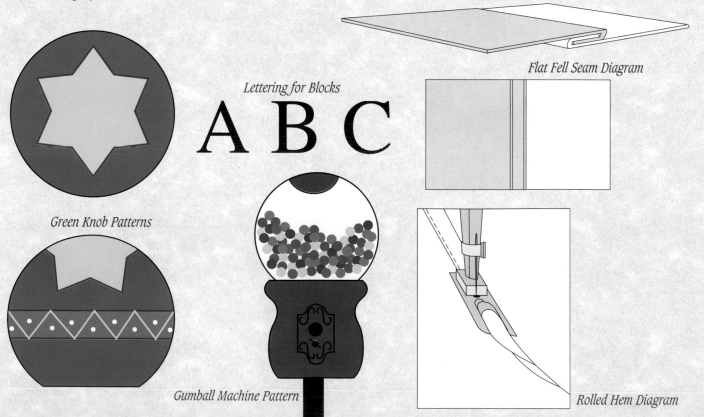

Lettering for Blocks

A B C

Green Knob Patterns

Gumball Machine Pattern

Flat Fell Seam Diagram

Rolled Hem Diagram

# Be a Clown

*Step*

T
squa
sure
whi
insi
rem

*Step*

U
déco
met
déco
App
and
Déc

*Step*

D
to s
thre
mus
thre
wag
ont
insi
win
hol
mo
is c

*Step*

l
Glu
dril

*Step*

C
pat
inv
stra
har
ver
is 3
edg
1¹⁄

# Memories

## Materials Needed

### For the Base, Including Music Box Accessories:
Pine for lid, 5$^1$/$_2$" wide x 5$^1$/$_2$" deep x $^1$/$_2$" thick
Pine for bottom, 4$^1$/$_2$" wide x 4$^1$/$_2$" deep x $^1$/$_2$" thick
4 pieces of pine for sides,
   5" wide x 7$^1$/$_2$" deep x $^1$/$_2$" thick
Finishing nails
Two-by-two, 7" length
2 brass stop hinges, $^3$/$_4$"
18-note key-wind musical movement
T-bar winding key, $^3$/$_4$"
Pour-on polymer coating, 8 fluid ounces
Sandpaper
Wood filler

### Decorative Accessories for Music Box Pictured:
Ceramic cat head, 5" high x 9$^1$/$_4$" diameter
6 greeting cards, 5" x 7"
9 gold-tone jingle bells, 6mm
Rhinestone crystal, 8mm x 12mm
Gray crinkled crepe or silk fabric, 2$^1$/$_2$" x 44"
Pink crinkled crepe or silk fabric, 2" x 44"
Plum velvet, 8" x 16"
3$^1$/$_2$"-wide ivory lace, 1 yard
4mm green silk ribbon, 1 yard
4mm off-white silk ribbon, 1 yard
4mm plum silk ribbon, 1 yard
Ivory quilting thread
Invisible thread

### Acrylic Paint Colors:
Black
Brownish-yellow
Coral
Dark gray
Green
Medium gray
Off-white
Yellow-green

*Diagram*

### Adhesives and Spray Sealer:
Industrial-strength glue
Super glue
Tacky glue
Wood glue
Gloss spray sealer

### Tools and Brushes:
Cardboard
Drill with $^1$/$_4$" drill bit
Hammer
Needle
Paintbrushes
Paper towels
Ruler
Scissors
Sewing machine
Spackling knife
X-acto knife

## Step-by-Step Assembly

### Step One:
Using wood glue, glue two box sides together and use finishing nails to secure. Refer to diagram at left. Glue on next side and nail. Repeat with last side. Glue and nail in box bottom — this will square up the box. Allow to dry thoroughly.

### Step Two:
Using wood filler and a spackling knife, fill in box joints and nail holes. Allow to dry thoroughly. Using sandpaper, sand box and lid. Refer to instructions for Sanding on page 14.

### Step Three:
Using a paintbrush, paint box and lid with medium gray acrylic paint. Refer to instructions for Painting on page 14.

### Step Four:
Using a ruler and an X-acto knife, cut four greeting cards at center fold to measure 5" wide x 7" high. Cut two greeting cards to measure 5" x 5" for the lid.

### Step Five:
Using Tacky glue, apply a thin layer to the back of one greeting card at a time. Carefully center cards on box sides. Smooth out air bubbles. Repeat with lid. Allow to dry thoroughly.

# Index